Supporting Air and Expeditionary Forces

Analysis of Maintenance Forward Support Location Operations

Amanda Geller, David George, Robert S. Tripp,
Mahyar A. Amouzegar, C. Robert Roll, Jr.

Prepared for the United States Air Force

PROJECT AIR FORCE

The research reported here was sponsored by the United States Air Force under contract F49642-01-C-0003. Further information may be obtained from the Strategic Planning Division, Directorate of Plans, Hq USAF.

Library of Congress Cataloging-in-Publication Data

Supporting air and space expeditionary forces : analysis of maintenance forward support location operations / Amanda Geller ... [et al.].
     p. cm.
     "MG-151."
     Includes bibliographical references.
     ISBN 0-8330-3572-X (pbk. : alk. paper)
     1. United States. Air Force—Supplies and stores. 2. Airplanes, Military—United States—Maintenance and repair. 3. United States. Air Force—Facilities. 4. United States. Air Force—Foreign service. I. Geller, Amanda.

UG1123.D87 2004
358.4'183—dc22

2004007916

Cover and interior photos courtesy of Major Ray Lindsay, 48 Component Maintenance Squadron Commander, USAF.

The RAND Corporation is a nonprofit research organization providing objective analysis and effective solutions that address the challenges facing the public and private sectors around the world. RAND's publications do not necessarily reflect the opinions of its research clients and sponsors.

RAND® is a registered trademark.

Published 2004 by the RAND Corporation
1700 Main Street, P.O. Box 2138, Santa Monica, CA 90407-2138
1200 South Hayes Street, Arlington, VA 22202-5050
201 North Craig Street, Suite 202, Pittsburgh, PA 15213-1516
RAND URL: http://www.rand.org/
To order RAND documents or to obtain additional information, contact
Distribution Services: Telephone: (310) 451-7002;
Fax: (310) 451-6915; Email: order@rand.org

Preface

During the past six years, the RAND Corporation has studied options for configuring an Agile Combat Support (ACS) system that would enable the Air and Space Expeditionary Force (AEF) goals of rapid deployment, immediate employment, and uninterrupted sustainment from a force structure located primarily within the continental United States (CONUS). This report is one of a series that addresses ACS options; it discusses the conceptual development and recent implementation of maintenance forward support locations (FSLs, also known as Centralized Intermediate Repair Facilities [CIRFs]) for the United States Air Force. The analysis focuses on the years leading up to and including the Air Force CIRF test, which tested the operations of centralized intermediate repair facilities in the European theater from September 2001 to February 2002.

The research reported here was sponsored by the Air Force Deputy Chief of Staff for Installations and Logistics (AF/IL) and conducted in the Resource Management Program of RAND Project AIR FORCE. The analysis was completed in June 2002.

This report should be of interest to logisticians, operators, and mobility planners throughout the Department of Defense (DoD), especially those in the Air Force. Other publications in the series include:

- *Supporting Expeditionary Aerospace Forces: An Integrated Strategic Agile Combat Support Planning Framework*, Robert S. Tripp et al. (MR-1056-AF). This report describes an integrated combat support planning framework that may be used to evaluate support options on a continuing basis, particularly as technology, force structure, and threats change.

- *Supporting Expeditionary Aerospace Forces: New Agile Combat Support Postures,* Lionel Galway et al. (MR-1075-AF). This report describes how alternative resourcing of forward operating locations (FOLs) can support employment timelines for future AEF operations. It finds that rapid employment for combat requires some prepositioning of resources at FOLs.

- *Supporting Expeditionary Aerospace Forces: An Analysis of F-15 Avionics Options,* Eric Peltz et al. (MR-1174-AF). This report examines alternatives for meeting F-15 avionics maintenance requirements across a range of likely scenarios. The authors evaluate investments for new F-15 Avionics Intermediate Shop test equipment against several support options, including deploying maintenance capabilities with units, performing maintenance at FSLs, or performing all maintenance at the home station for deploying units.

- *Supporting Expeditionary Aerospace Forces: A Concept for Evolving to the Agile Combat Support/Mobility System of the Future,* Robert S. Tripp et al. (MR-1179-AF). This report describes the vision for the ACS system of the future based on individual commodity study results.

- *Supporting Expeditionary Aerospace Forces: Expanded Analysis of LANTIRN Options,* Amatzia Feinberg et al. (MR-1225-AF). This report examines alternatives for meeting Low Altitude Navigation and Targeting Infrared for Night (LANTIRN) support requirements for AEF operations. The authors evaluate investments for new LANTIRN test equipment against several support options, including deploying maintenance capabilities with units, performing maintenance at FSLs, or performing all maintenance at CONUS support hubs for deploying units.

- *Supporting Expeditionary Aerospace Forces: Lessons From the Air War Over Serbia,* Amatzia Feinberg et al. (MR-1263-AF). This report describes how the Air Force's ad hoc implementation of many elements of an expeditionary ACS structure to support the air war over Serbia offered opportunities to assess how well these elements actually supported combat operations and what the results imply for the configuration of the Air Force ACS structure. The findings support the efficacy of the emerging expeditionary ACS structural framework and the associated but still-evolving Air Force support strategies. (This report is not releasable to the general public.)

- *Supporting Expeditionary Aerospace Forces: Alternatives for Jet Engine Intermediate Maintenance*, Mahyar A. Amouzegar et al. (MR-1431-AF). This report evaluates the manner in which Jet Engine Intermediate Maintenance (JEIM) shops can best be configured to facilitate overseas deployments. The authors examine a number of JEIM support options, which are distinguished primarily by the degree to which JEIM support is centralized or decentralized.

- *Supporting Expeditionary Aerospace Forces: A Combat Support Command and Control Architecture for Supporting the Expeditionary Aerospace Force*, James Leftwich et al. (MR-1536-AF). This report outlines the framework for evaluating options for combat support execution planning and control. The analysis describes the combat support command and control operational architecture as it is now and as it should be in the future. It also describes the changes that must take place to achieve that future state.

- *Supporting Expeditionary Aerospace Forces: Reconfiguring Footprint to Speed Expeditionary Aerospace Forces Deployment*, Lionel A. Galway et al. (MR-1625-AF). This report develops an analysis framework--footprint configuration—to assist in devising and evaluating strategies for footprint reduction. The authors attempt to define footprint and to establish a way to monitor its reduction.

RAND Project AIR FORCE

RAND Project AIR FORCE (PAF), a division of the RAND Corporation, is the U.S. Air Force's federally funded research and development center for studies and analyses. PAF provides the Air Force with independent analyses of policy alternatives affecting the development, employment, combat readiness, and support of current and future aerospace forces. Research is performed in four programs: Aerospace Force Development; Manpower, Personnel, and Training; Resource Management; and Strategy and Doctrine.

Additional information about PAF is available on our web site at http://www.rand.org/paf.

Contents

Figures

Tables

Summary

Since 1990, the United States military has been called upon to support crises that range from Operation Desert Storm to humanitarian relief operations. These operations create a diverse and unpredictable set of sortie-generation needs, from air-to-ground combat to the transport of food and supplies. To meet these demands, the Air Force is reorganizing into an Air and Space Expeditionary Force (AEF). Behind this new vision of force management is the idea that forces able to deploy quickly and frequently from the continental United States can replace the permanent forward presence of airpower that the Air Force employed during the Cold War.

However, deploying airpower quickly and frequently strains the Air Force's current combat support system. The original concept of the AEF called for deploying the entire combat and support infrastructure from the continental United States. However, the resources needed to support a combat deployment are heavy, and require significant airlift and time to move to the theater. Furthermore, the need to redeploy the entire support structure with each combat deployment limits flexibility and creates instability among personnel. The Air Force is consequently reexamining its support infrastructure to focus on new goals: faster deployment, reduction in the mass of materiel to move, increased flexibility, and greater personnel stability. This study examines one potential reconfiguration of the Air Force's current support system: the creation of maintenance Forward Support Locations (FSLs) to consolidate intermediate maintenance near, but not in, the theater of operations.

Centralizing the Intermediate-Maintenance Infrastructure: Forward Support Locations and the AEF

Over the past sixty years, a range of factors—from historical events and operating environments to personnel, equipment, and spares constraints—has led Air Force support policy to oscillate between two types of infrastructure: decentralized and centralized. In a decentralized maintenance structure, each unit or wing maintains the ability to make intermediate repairs to its own assets at its main operating base. A centralized infrastructure, on the other hand, calls for numerous units to share one or more maintenance facilities, either in theater, at other locations overseas, or in the continental United States. Combat units at forward locations send items needing intermediate maintenance to these facilities, where they are repaired and then returned to the units.

The unpredictability of the AEF environment has led RAND and the Air Force to call for a support infrastructure flexible enough to be tailored to meet the demands of any contingency. RAND calls its vision of a new structure an Agile Combat Support (ACS) network. Within this vision, intermediate-maintenance activities, which are performed away from the aircraft at base shops, offer potential for significant change. Centralizing these activities has the potential to improve overall support performance.

The Air Force has studied centralized intermediate-maintenance facilities on several occasions, and has implemented them at times in tests and real-world operations. The appeal and effectiveness of centralization have depended on a variety of factors, including operational needs, availability of maintenance equipment, and risk to deployed units. The development of ACS in the 1990s presented another environment in which centralized intermediate maintenance indicated the potential to improve operations. RAND conducted several analyses to determine the effectiveness of Centralized Intermediate Repair Facility (CIRF) support for a series of commodities: F-15 avionics components, LANTIRN pods, and jet engines. In addition, RAND examined potential locations for CIRFs, the concept of deployment footprint (a key metric of CIRF efficiency), and the command and control system used to support repair and other processes. (See p. 36.)

While all maintenance options, ranging from complete decentralization to centralization of repair functions in a single facility, involve tradeoffs between reliance on transportation and command and control, the availability of support resources, and other factors, our research has shown that centralization of intermediate maintenance at FSLs (which the Air Force calls CIRFs) has the potential to help the Air Force reduce its deployment timelines, increase flexibility, and otherwise meet its expeditionary goals.

In 1999, the Air Force implemented CIRFs on an ad hoc basis during the Air War Over Serbia (AWOS). Centralizing intermediate-maintenance activities provided an effective level of support, at far lower equipment and personnel deployment levels than those required by decentralized repair. However, the ad hoc implementation led to complications and delays in decisionmaking. The Air Force determined that a formal test would allow a comprehensive look at CIRF operations without the difficulties faced during the AWOS.

The Air Force CIRF Test

RAND's research in the 1990s and the performance of maintenance FSLs during the AWOS contributed to the Air Force's decision to formally test the centralized intermediate-maintenance concept. The Air Force directorate of Installations and Logistics (AF/IL) developed a detailed concept of operations and test plan that defined the roles and responsibilities of European CIRFs in supporting steady-state operations in Southwest Asia, from September 2001 through February 2002.

The six-month CIRF test demonstrated that centralized intermediate maintenance was capable of supporting steady-state operations with a reduced deployment footprint. Furthermore, the command and control network supporting CIRF operations allowed the system to recognize when operational goals were in jeopardy and to adapt support resources to meet the required sortie schedule. In short, the test proved that centralized intermediate repair could help the Air Force meet its goals of faster deployment, smaller footprint, and reduced personnel, equipment, and force protection requirements.

At the same time, the CIRF test pinpointed several opportunities for improvement. Deployment management and transportation problems led to delays in CIRF operations, and shortfalls in command and control led to confusion of responsibilities and difficulties in effectively allocating resources. The Air Force has undertaken studies to improve both of these systems. (See p. 60.)

Next Steps in Implementing the Agile Combat Support Network

Despite the considerable achievements of the CIRF test, other issues must be addressed if the Air Force wants to implement a truly global ACS system. For example, under certain circumstances, CIRFs located in the continental United States might provide the best intermediate-maintenance support. Accordingly, the Air Force has begun to examine the requirements for establishing CIRFs at domestic sites. Furthermore, several questions about the ownership of assets need to be resolved for the Air Force to attain the full benefits of FSLs. Currently units "own" their assets, which prevents pooling of assets at FSLs or other locations where they are needed most. Changing the current policy to centralize ownership of maintenance equipment, facilities, and components will enable FSLs to operate more effectively. However, this centralization will require modifications to the current command and control organizational structure to ensure centralized decisionmaking that will help units meet their operational requirements. (See p. 88.)

This report reviews much of the research and testing that show the advantages maintenance FSLs offer as part of a full ACS system and discusses the problems that remain and how they might be resolved.

Acknowledgments

Many persons inside and outside the Air Force provided valuable assistance and support to our work. We thank Lieutenant General Michael Zettler for initiating this study, and Ms. Susan O'Neal and Mr. Michael Aimone for their ongoing support.

Major General Terry Gabreski has been instrumental in the development and implementation of the centralized intermediate repair concept. Her support of the CIRF concept before, during, and after the Air War Over Serbia strongly influenced the maintenance structure of the Air Force and paved the way for CIRF implementation.

We would also like to thank the Air Force Installations and Logistics Maintenance directorate (AF/ILM) for its guidance and insight throughout the CIRF test. Major Patrick Kumashiro (AF/ILMM) played a key role in developing the CIRF test plan, measuring performance throughout the test, and advocating the CIRF concept throughout the Air Force community. We would also like to thank Mr. Sam Pennartz (AF/IL), Ms. Lydia Newsom (AF/ILMY), Col Steven Aylor (AF/ILMM), Lt Col Robert Wood (AF/ILMY), and Mr. Vernon Hilderbrand (AF/ILMY).

We had extensive help from MAJCOM engine staff, particularly Lt Col John Cooper (ACC/LGMP), CMSgt Michael Kinser (ACC/LGMP) and Mr. Thomas Smith (ACC/LGMP) at Langley AFB, and CMSgt Duane Mackey (USAFE/LGM) at Ramstein AB, who fielded numerous questions, allowed us access to data, and provided valuable insight about the engine repair process. We would also like to thank Mr. Chris Szczepan (OC-ALC/R) at Tinker AFB, for his help with engine data and requirements.

We also would like to thank CMSgt Florencio Garza (ACC/LGMA) and CMSgt Craun Fansler (USAFE/LGMAS) for their information on avionics pod requirements and repair processes and for access to unit flying programs. We also appreciate the help of the RAMPOD staff at Warner Robbins Air Logistics Center, for access to pod reliability and repair data.

For information on the Regional Supply Squadron and CIRF command and control, we would like to thank Lt Col Joseph Codispoti (AF/ILGP). We also appreciate the help of the USAFE/RSS staff, including Lt Col Frederick, Captain Cotto, MSgt Dean Olney, and MSgt Jeff Strickland.

We also appreciate the information provided by CMSgt Frank Levand, MSgt Terry White, CMSgt Robert Cushing, MSgt Terrill Choy, and SMSgt Dave Westwood in our visit to the Spangdahlem CIRF.

At RAND, we benefited greatly from the knowledge and support of many of our colleagues, including (in alphabetical order) Stephen Brady, Edward Chan, John Drew, Lionel Galway, Christopher Hanks, Kip Miller, Patrick Mills, and Hy Shulman. We greatly appreciate the input of Susan Bohandy, whose thorough and thoughtful critique contributed greatly to the clarity of this paper. We also benefited from careful reviews by John Halliday and Jim Masters.

As always, the analysis and conclusions are the responsibility of the authors.

Acronyms

AAF	Army Air Force
AB	Air Base
ACC	Air Combat Command
ACS	Agile Combat Support
AEF	Air and Space Expeditionary Force
AEW	Aerospace Expeditionary Wing
AFB	Air Force Base
AF/IL	Air Force Installations and Logistics
AFLC	Air Force Logistics Command
AFLMA	Air Force Logistics Management Agency
AIS	Avionics Intermediate Shop
AMC	Air Mobility Command
ANG	Air National Guard
AOR	Area of Responsibility
APOD	Aerial Port of Debarkation
ASC	Air Service Command
ASD	Average Sortie Duration
ASETF	Aerospace Expeditionary Task Force
AWM	Awaiting Maintenance

AWOS	Air War Over Serbia
AWP	Awaiting Parts
C2	Command and Control
CC	Combatant Commander
CENTAF	Central Command Air Forces
CENTCOM	U.S. Central Command
CEP	CIRF Engine Pool
CHPMSK	Contingency High Priority Mission Spares Kits
CIRF	Centralized Intermediate Repair Facility
CLR	Chief of Staff Logistics Review
CONOPS	Concept of Operations
CONUS	Continental United States
COP	Common Operating Picture
CRC	Consolidated Repair Concept
CRS	Component Repair Squadron
CS	Combat Support
CSAF	Chief of Staff, U.S. Air Force
CSC2	Combat Support Command and Control
CSL	CONUS Support Location
CWT	Customer Wait Time
DS/DS	Desert Shield/Desert Storm
EAF	Expeditionary Aerospace Force
ECM	Electronic Countermeasure
EDS	European Distribution System
EUCOM	European Command
FMC	Fully Mission Capable
FOD	Foreign Object Damage
FOL	Forward Operating Location

FSL	Forward Support Location
FSS	Field Service Station
GAO	General Accounting Office
GIC	Global Integration Center
ILM	Intermediate-Level Maintenance
INW	In Work
IOR	Initial Operating Requirement
ITV	In-Transit Visibility
JCS	Joint Chiefs of Staff
JEIM	Jet Engine Intermediate Maintenance
LANTIRN	Low-Altitude Navigation and Targeting Infrared for Night
LGM	Logistics Group Maintenance
LRU	Line Replaceable Unit
MAJCOM	Major Command
MDS	Mission Design Series
METRIC	Multi-Echelon Technique for Recoverable Item Control
METS	Mobile Electronic Test Set
MICAP	Mission Capability
MOB	Main Operating Base
MOE	Measure of Effectiveness
MPIP	Maintenance Posture Improvement Program
MRC	Major Regional Conflict
MSB	Main Support Base
NAF	Numbered Air Force
NMC	Not Mission Capable
OCAC	Office of the Chief of Air Corps
OCONUS	Out of CONUS
OEF	Operation Enduring Freedom

OIF	Operation Iraqi Freedom
ONW	Operation Northern Watch
OSC	Operational Support Center
OSW	Operation Southern Watch
PAA	Primary Aircraft Assigned
PACAF	Pacific Air Forces
PMEL	Precision Measurement Equipment Laboratory
POC	Point of Contact
PRS	Propulsion Requirements System
RAF	Royal Air Force
RCM	Reliability Centered Maintenance
REMCO	Rear-Echelon Maintenance Combined Operations
RR	Removal Rate (removals/1000 flying hr)
RSP	Readiness Spares Package
RSS	Regional Supply Squadron
SAC	Strategic Air Command
SEAD	Suppression of Enemy Air Defenses
SWA	Southwest Asia
TAC	Tactical Air Command
TACC	Tanker Airlift Control Center
TCN	Transportation Control Number
TCTO	Time Change Technical Order
TDS	Theater Distribution System
TRANSCOM	Transportation Command
TT	Transportation Time (one-way to/from CIRF)
ULN	Unit Line Number
USAFE	United States Air Forces in Europe
UTC	Unit Type Code

UTE	Utilization rate (sorties/aircraft/month)
WRM	War Reserve Materiel
XOP	Director of EAF Implementation
ZI	Zone of the Interior

CHAPTER ONE

Introduction

The United States security environment has changed dramatically in recent years. Since the Gulf War in 1991, the U.S. military has been called upon to respond to an almost nonstop series of full-scale crises and lesser contingencies, ranging in scope from coercive air strikes in Bosnia, to humanitarian operations in Africa, to shows of force in the Middle East. The Air Force has played an instrumental role in all of these operations, staging scores of deployments, often with short lead times, in far-flung locations and against uncertain adversaries.[1]

In contrast, during the Cold War, the United States faced a few known enemies in two principal theaters, Europe and Southeast Asia. The basing structure was well established, and enough equipment and personnel resources were available to support every deployment. However, since the early 1990s, as the number of contingencies has proliferated, the force has become smaller, the pool of deployable resources has decreased, and there has been a drawdown in overseas basing. Today the Air Force has to do much more with much less.

---

[1] For example, in fiscal year 1999, USAF operations included 38,000 sorties associated with Operation Allied Force, 19,000 sorties to enforce the no-fly zones in Iraq, and some 70,000 mobility missions to more than 140 countries (see Sweetman, 2000).

Creation of the Air and Space Expeditionary Force

To respond more effectively to these new demands, the Air Force intends to reorganize into an Air and Space Expeditionary Force (AEF).[2] This reorganization will generate a force that, when a crisis occurs, can deploy quickly from the continental United States (CONUS) to anywhere in the world, commence operations rapidly, and sustain those operations as needed. The underlying premise is that rapid deployment from CONUS and a seamless transition to sustainment can substitute for an ongoing U.S. presence in theater, greatly reducing or even eliminating deployments the Air Force would otherwise stage for the purpose of deterrence.

To implement the AEF concept, the Air Force created ten Aerospace Expeditionary Forces,[3] each composed of a mixture of fighters, bombers, and tankers. These ten AEFs respond to contingencies on a rotating basis: For 90 days, two of the ten AEFs must be ready to respond to any crisis needing airpower. This vulnerable period is followed by a 12-month period during which those two AEFs are not subject to short-notice deployments or rotations. In the AEF system, individual wings and squadrons no longer deploy and fight as a full and/or single unit as they did during the Cold War. Instead, each AEF customizes a force package for each contingency, using varying numbers of aircraft from different units. This fixed schedule of steady-state rotational deployments promises to increase flexibility by enabling the Air Force to respond immediately to any crisis with little or no effect on other deployments.

The dramatic increase in deployments from CONUS combined with the reduction of Air Force resource levels have increased the

---

[2] The Air Force defines "expeditionary" as conducting "global aerospace operations with forces based primarily in the US that will deploy rapidly to begin operations on beddown." U.S. Air Force, *EAF Factsheet*, June 1999.

[3] Henceforth, when it is clear from the context, we will use AEF to represent both the concept and the force package.

need for effective combat support.[4] Because combat support resources are heavy and constitute a large portion of deployments (as shown in Figure 1.1), they have the potential to enable or constrain operational goals, particularly in today's environment, which is dependent on rapid deployment.[5] Consequently, the Air Force is reexamining its combat support infrastructure to focus on faster deployment, smaller footprint, greater personnel stability, and increased flexibility.

An aspect of combat support that offers the potential for substantial improvement is the intermediate-level maintenance of end items, such as engines and electronic warfare pods. This report focuses on the evolution of Air Force approaches to intermediate maintenance, and how these differing approaches may affect the Air Force's ability to meet the operational demands of the AEF.

Two Operating Concepts for Intermediate Maintenance

For decades, opinions within the Air Force have differed considerably on what approach to intermediate maintenance would provide the greatest benefits. Over the past sixty years, a range of factors—from historical events and operating environments to personnel, equipment, and spares constraints and the preference of leaders—has led Air Force policy to oscillate between two concepts of operation: decentralized and centralized.[6] In a decentralized system of intermediate maintenance, each unit or wing maintains the ability to make intermediate repairs to end items from its own assets at its main operating

---

[4] Air Force doctrine defines combat support to include "the actions taken to ready, sustain, and protect aerospace personnel, assets, and capabilities through all peacetime and wartime military operations."

[5] Theater assets are provided by organizations outside the combat unit itself. In the case shown in Figure 1.1, most theater materiel was provided by CENTAF (Central Command Air Forces).

[6] This report uses the terms "decentralized" and "centralized" to refer to the physical infrastructure of intermediate repair facilities, not to the command structure within and between maintenance organizations.

Figure 1.1
Support Footprint for Aerospace Power Is Substantial

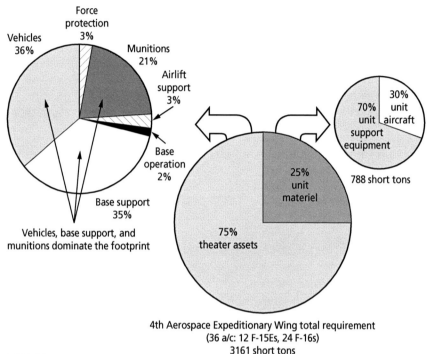

4th Aerospace Expeditionary Wing total requirement
(36 a/c: 12 F-15Es, 24 F-16s)
3161 short tons

RAND MG151-1.1

base. Hence, decentralization is also referred to as base "self-sufficiency."

In contrast, a centralized system of intermediate maintenance calls for numerous units to share one or more intermediate-maintenance facilities—either in theater, at other locations overseas, or in the CONUS. Rather than taking along equipment and personnel to conduct intermediate repairs locally, combat units at forward locations send items needing intermediate maintenance back to centralized facilities, where they are repaired and then returned to the units.

Intermediate-Maintenance Strategies During and After the Cold War

Throughout the Cold War, the Air Force favored a form of decentralized intermediate maintenance in which a combat unit would deploy with enough equipment and personnel from its main operating base to ensure that it could perform repairs at forward locations.[7] Centralized maintenance facilities were implemented on occasion but only under particular circumstances—when resources were constrained, for example, or strategic considerations required maintenance staff to be moved from the Area of Responsibility (AOR).

The unpredictability of the post–Cold War environment brought a serious challenge to the traditional decentralized intermediate-maintenance infrastructure. Initial AEF goals specified a 48-hour deployment timeline to anywhere in the world. *Air Force Vision 2020* states, "We will be able to deploy an AEF in 48 hours, fast enough to curb many crises before they escalate."[8] In terms of raw flying time, this goal is attainable: If the two on-call AEFs have aircraft and crews ready for action, combat aircraft can feasibly deploy to forward locations within 48 hours.

However, to get intermediate maintenance up and running, this timeline is not realistic. The time needed to move the bulky, heavy equipment required for intermediate maintenance can easily exceed what operational demands allow. Furthermore, transporting the large volume of needed materiel consumes airlift resources that might be better used for another aspect of the deployment. The demand for trained personnel for all of the deployments being staged at any given time may leave units short staffed, and if an intermediate-maintenance resource package is not tailored to the needs of a specific force package, the Air Force runs a considerable risk of deploying

---

[7] Strictly speaking, no unit or base is fully self-sufficient—many reparables are beyond base-repair capability. Moreover, at the time, doctrine required deployment with 30 days of spares and equipment plus time to set up intermediate repair capabilities. However, none of the plans envisioned a 48- or even 96-hour deployment and employment plan.

[8] *Air Force Vision 2020: Global Vigilance, Reach, and Power* (Washington, D.C., 2001) lays out how the Air Force plans to support the national strategy.

more resources than are necessary or duplicating resources at a forward location. These issues undermine the Air Force's ability to deploy and employ rapidly and efficiently, maintain a full pool of well-trained intermediate-maintenance personnel, and operate with the greatest possible flexibility.

RAND's Concept of Agile Combat Support

Since the end of the Cold War and the inception of the AEF concept, RAND has worked with the Air Force to determine options for intermediate maintenance, and for combat support as a whole, that can meet the Air Force's changing needs. RAND's research has resulted in what it calls an Agile Combat Support (ACS) network, consisting of five principal elements:

1. *Forward Operating Locations (FOLs)* are sites in a theater out of which tactical forces operate. FOLs can have differing levels of combat support resources to support a variety of employment timelines. Some FOLs in critical areas under high threat should have equipment prepositioned to enable aerospace packages designed for heavy combat to deploy rapidly. These FOLs might be augmented by other, more austere FOLs that would take longer to spin up. In parts of the world where conflict is less likely or humanitarian missions are the norm, all FOLs might be austere.
2. *Forward Support Locations (FSLs)* are sites near or within the theater of operation for storage of heavy combat support resources such as munitions or War Reserve Materiel (WRM), or sites for consolidated maintenance and other support activities. The configuration and specific functions of FSLs depend on their geographic location, the threat level, steady-state and potential wartime requirements, and the costs and benefits associated with using these facilities.
3. *CONUS Support Locations (CSLs)* are support facilities in the continental United States. CONUS depots are one type of CSL, as are contractor facilities. Other types of CSLs may be analogous to

FSLs. Such structures are needed to support CONUS forces should repair capability and other activities be removed from units. These activities may be set up at major Air Force bases, appropriate civilian transportation hubs, or Air Force or other defense repair and/or supply depots.

4. *A transportation network* connects the FOLs and FSLs with each other and CONUS, including en route tanker support. It is essential to an ACS system in which FSLs need assured transportation links to support expeditionary forces. FSLs themselves could be transportation hubs.

5. *A Combat Support Command and Control (CSC2) system* facilitates a variety of critical management tasks: (1) estimating support requirements, (2) configuring the nodes of the system selected to support a given contingency, (3) executing support activities, (4) measuring actual combat support performance against planned performance, (5) developing recourse plans when the system is not within control limits, and (6) reacting swiftly to rapidly changing circumstances.

This report focuses on FSLs used for centralized intermediate maintenance of end items. The Air Force refers to these repair FSLs as Centralized Intermediate Repair Facilities, or CIRFs. Although a CIRF may be located at an FOL, a CSL, or an FSL—that is, located either abroad or in the CONUS—when we use the term CIRF in this report, we will be referring specifically to FSLs. We will refer to CONUS CIRFs explicitly as such.

RAND's ACS framework is illustrated in Figure 1.2.[9] In its ideal state, this infrastructure is tailorable to the demands of any contingency. The first three parts—FOLs, FSLs, and CSLs—are variable; the Air Force configures them as deployments occur to best meet specific needs. In contrast, the last two elements—a reliable

---

[9] This is a different system from the austere "bring-it-all-from-CONUS" system implicitly envisioned during early discussions of the Expeditionary Air Force (EAF). Note that "bringing it all" really entailed deploying with unit materiel as described in Figure 1.1.

Figure 1.2
Elements of the ACS Network

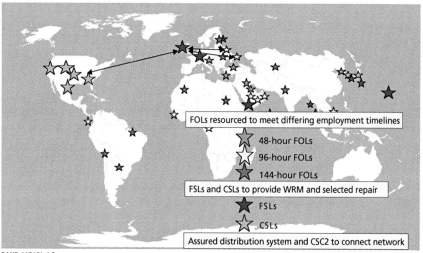

FOLs resourced to meet differing employment timelines

48-hour FOLs

96-hour FOLs

144-hour FOLs

FSLs and CSLs to provide WRM and selected repair

FSLs

CSLs

Assured distribution system and CSC2 to connect network

RAND *MG151–1.2*

transportation network and CSC2—are indispensable ingredients in any con figuration. Determining how to distribute responsibility for the support activities for any given operation among CSLs, FSLs, and FOLs is the essence of strategic support decisions. For example, in determining the number of FSLs to support a given operation, and their role, the Air Force must carefully evaluate such factors as the support capability of available FSLs and the risks and costs of prepositioning specific resources at those locations.

The relationship between maintenance FSLs and the FOLs they support is diagrammed in Figure 1.3. Combat aircraft operate out of FOLs until they require maintenance. Simple maintenance (e.g., removing a broken end item and replacing it with a spare, called "on-equipment maintenance") can be conducted at the FOL. When an end item needs intermediate maintenance that cannot be conducted at the FOL (called "off-equipment maintenance" because technicians must remove the part from the airplane to fix it), it is sent to the FSL, repaired, and then returned. This movement between operating and

Figure 1.3
FOL/FSL Operational Concept

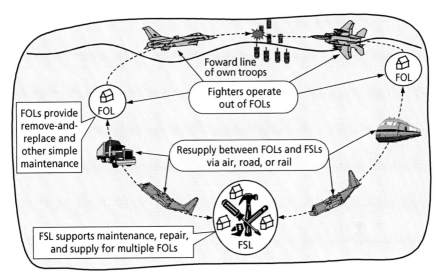

Foward line of own troops

Fighters operate out of FOLs

FOL

FOL

FOLs provide remove-and-replace and other simple maintenance

FOL

Resupply between FOLs and FSLs via air, road, or rail

FSL supports maintenance, repair, and supply for multiple FOLs

FSL

support sites underscores the dependence of the ACS system on effective distribution and CSC2.

Over the past six years, RAND has conducted a series of studies evaluating how utilizing the ACS system for intermediate maintenance compared with other possible intermediate-maintenance infrastructures (for example, either decentralized or based entirely in CONUS) in meeting the Air Force's changing needs.

Among the earliest of RAND's studies were analyses of how different infrastructures would support intermediate maintenance of several commodities, including Low-Altitude Navigation and Targeting Infrared for Night (LANTIRN) and electronic countermeasure (ECM) pods,[10] F-15 avionics,[11] and jet engines.[12] RAND followed these studies with an evaluation of the risk and base-access issues as-

---

[10] Feinberg et al., 2001.

[11] Peltz et al., 2000.

[12] Amouzegar et al., 2001.

sociated with centralized maintenance. It then looked at lessons learned from CIRF operations during the Air War Over Serbia (AWOS). Lessons learned from the AWOS resulted in further research that examined CSC2 and the measure of deployment footprint, both of which are critical to the success and evaluation of maintenance FSL operations.

The outcomes of these analyses have demonstrated that there is no single "right" answer to the question of intermediate-maintenance infrastructure. All options involve tradeoffs between intratheater transportation, and C2 systems, additional spares, and other support resources. Different historical conditions, operating environments, deployment goals, levels of resource availability, and other factors make different options look more attractive at any given time.

Our research has shown that in the current environment, the ACS system, leveraging principles of centralized intermediate maintenance, can help the Air Force meet its AEF goals. Given reliable transportation to enable distribution and effective CSC2, maintenance FSLs have the potential to improve deployment speed and flexibility, reduce footprint, and reduce the personnel and equipment requirements in an AOR.

The Air Force's Active Involvement in CIRF Operations

The conclusions and recommendations set forth in the early RAND studies on the tradeoffs between different intermediate-maintenance infrastructures played a role in the Air Force's decision to establish CIRFs during the AWOS in 1999. The implementation of CIRFs in the war resulted in effective maintenance operations with a reduced deployment footprint. However, the ad hoc implementation of the Air Force's transportation[13] and C2 system presented operational challenges.

---

[13] Although transportation is primarily a Transportation Command (TRANSCOM) responsibility, this responsibility was delegated to the Air Force during AWOS as they had the preponderance of force.

Lessons learned from the AWOS led the Air Force to implement a formal test of CIRF operations in which the Air Force properly exercised the transportation and C2 elements of CIRF support.

Realizing the Vision of a Global ACS System

To implement a truly global ACS system, a number of issues remain to be addressed. Because of manpower constraints, the Air Force has been considering the implementation of CIRFs in CONUS as well as overseas. As of January 2004, these proposals are still under study. Our analyses have also shown that if CIRF-based alternatives are ultimately to work effectively, the Air Force must ensure a reliable CSC2 system and transportation network.

In addition, several issues about the ownership of assets need to be resolved to fully attain the benefits of FSLs. Currently, units "own" their assets, which prevents pooling of assets at FSLs or other locations where they are needed most. Changes in decentralized-to-centralized ownership of maintenance equipment, facilities, and components policies and a modified C2 organizational structure to support common ownership are needed.

Organization of This Report

This report reviews much of the research and testing that show the advantages maintenance FSLs offer. It also discusses the problems that remain and suggests ways to resolve them. Chapter Two describes Air Force studies and implementation of centralized intermediate maintenance over several decades. These historical precedents offer valuable lessons not only about when and how centralization can work, but about the issues centralization can involve. Chapter Three chronicles how the Air Force's demands have changed under the AEF construct and recent RAND research that supports the exploration of centralized repair. This research has indicated that centralized maintenance offers advantages in today's operating environment. Chapter Four describes the formal USAF CIRF test conducted between September 2001 and February 2002, the advantages demonstrated by CIRF operations, and the challenges they raise. Chapter Five discusses the development of the CIRF support tradespace, and Chapter Six presents our conclusions and recommendations for a broader implementation of the ACS system. The appendix describes the centralized ownership concept.

CHAPTER TWO

CIRF History

The Air Force's current interest in CIRFs is not unprecedented. In 1968, Major General Jack W. Waters, USAF (Ret.), then a lieutenant colonel, published an Air War College research report entitled, *The Development of Logistical Support Policies for Tactical Fighter Aircraft.* Lt Col Waters introduced his subject with a prophetic remark:

> The driving factor that has influenced the growing concern about logistics for tactical fighter forces has been the increased threat and actual involvement in non-nuclear wars in remote sections of the world. The capability to deploy tailored tactical forces to the threat area or areas and immediately employ their influence against an adversary or adversaries is, to a great extent, a function of the logistics concepts used by the available forces.[1]

Not only did Waters recognize what a crucial role logistics played in effective military operations, he also discerned, in a time dominated by the standoff between two nuclear superpowers, a mounting nonnuclear threat in inaccessible areas of the world. In these observations, Waters anticipated today's security environment and its concomitant need for far-flung, rapid deployments.

In his report, Waters recognized that where weapon system maintenance should take place, and who should be responsible for it were questions that could have several answers. At the time he was writing, it was standard practice for maintenance to take place at for-

---

[1] Waters, 1968, p. 2.

ward operating locations by a repair unit that would deploy with a fighting squadron. However, he suggested that a tactical force would be smaller, lighter, and consequently more mobile and less complex if it did not take with it all the equipment and personnel to equip it to perform complex maintenance. His report presented several alternatives for logistical support "for logisticians to consider when further change [from the standing policy was] contemplated."[2]

The alternative Waters preferred was "for some other organization [than a forward repair unit] to support the tactical fighter wing with ready to install serviceable components and engines."[3] He suggested that the Air Force Logistics Command (AFLC) role in base-level logistics support be expanded to encompass all maintenance for tactical fighters that needed to be performed away from the aircraft itself.[4] He also foresaw two-level maintenance and the roles that CSLs and FSLs could play as a permanent part of a worldwide logistics system for tactical fighter forces.

Waters' ideas were somewhat radical in a logistics environment dominated by commanders, operators, and technicians committed to keeping maintenance capability decentralized and who advocated a support policy that revolved around the principle of base self-sufficiency. Although two concepts of unit-level maintenance—decentralized and centralized—have coexisted since the early days of the Air Force, decentralization has dominated thinking about logistics since the beginning of the Cold War. For the past 50 years, official policy has favored decentralization, with efforts to explore alternatives often meeting strong resistance.

However, over time and under certain conditions, the Air Force has shown considerable interest in consolidating portions of its maintenance infrastructure, and on several occasions it has successfully done so. These historical precedents inform the current vision of a

[2] Waters, p. 59

[3] Waters, p. 65.

[4] This complex maintenance was referred to as "off-equipment maintenance," whereas more basic maintenance involving removal and reinstallation, rather than actual repair, of parts was known as "on-equipment maintenance."

CIRF-based system, showing both the real potential and the real challenges of implementing a consolidated (often called centralized) infrastructure for intermediate maintenance.

Shifts in Maintenance Policy in the Early Days of the Air Force

In its first two decades, the Air Force, then known as the U.S. Army Air Corps, took a centralized approach to logistics. From 1920 until 1942, the Materiel Division of the Office of the Chief of Air Corps was responsible for the logistical support of the Army Air Force (AAF). Through its Field Service Station (FSS), the Materiel Division managed supply and maintenance for the Air Corps. Four FSS depots conducted overhaul, aircraft repair, warehousing, and distribution of supplies. Supply and maintenance functions on Air Corps bases were under the direct control of the base commanders.[5]

As the Air Corps began to grow in the early 1940s, the problem of control over maintenance and supply on bases, as distinguished from depots, drew considerable attention. As early as November 1940, the FSS had proposed that control of supply and maintenance on all bases be assigned to the Materiel Division. This early proposal was rejected. When the Air Corps Maintenance Command was established in March 1941, the command's responsibility for maintenance stopped at the base boundary.[6]

Later in 1941, the Air Service Command (ASC) replaced the Air Corps Maintenance Command. Within CONUS,[7] all maintenance and supply above the first two echelons were placed under the supervision of the Chief of ASC. ASC established subdepots at CONUS

---

[5] Craven and Cate, 1955, pp. 363–364.

[6] Craven and Cate, p. 365.

[7] At the time, CONUS was referred to as the Zone of the Interior (ZI).

bases to carry out these new responsibilities. By September 1944, there were 238 subdepots.[8]

The combat and training commands never accepted the loss of their maintenance and supply responsibilities to ASC: Base commanders and nearly every level of command wanted operational units to be as self-sufficient as possible. In January 1944, the responsibility for operations of all subdepots within the United States was transferred from ASC to the bases supported by the subdepots. According to Waters, the efficiency of the subdepot system was degraded by this decision. Centralization was no longer a feasible policy.[9]

Overseas, the ASC never had control of logistical activities. Instead, each overseas command organized its own air service command to conduct third- and fourth-echelon supply and maintenance. AAF Regulation 65-1, August 14, 1942, defined and discussed the echelons of aircraft maintenance as follows: First echelon: That maintenance performed by the air echelon of the combat unit; second echelon: That maintenance performed by the ground echelon of the combat unit, air base squadrons, and airways detachments; third echelon: That maintenance performed by service groups and subdepots; fourth echelon: That maintenance performed by air depot groups and air depots. The paper attempted to make the point that outside of the ZI each overseas air force organized its own air service command to conduct third- and fourth-echelon maintenance and supply. Air depot groups were established in various theaters to conduct fourth-echelon operations. Service groups undertaking third-echelon maintenance and supply operations were mostly located on or near the combat bases being supported. Overseas air service commands became primarily concerned with fourth-echelon maintenance. The third echelon of maintenance and supply became identifiable as the field maintenance performed by units/shops under the subsequent three-level maintenance concept. Fourth-echelon operations were centralized, conducted by air depot groups established in

---

[8] Craven and Cate, pp. 367–388.

[9] Craven and Cate, pp. 367–368.

the various theaters. However, given continual disputes over control of third-echelon operations, combat units eventually began to perform their own third-echelon maintenance and supply.[10]

These early struggles set a precedent for the years to come. From that time until today, the strong desire among commanders for self-sufficiency has stood in opposition to efforts to centralize maintenance away from units. Staunch advocates of decentralization have argued that centralization reduces base self-sufficiency and that the risks—mostly associated with transportation and availability of serviceable parts—are too great.

Developments During the Korean War: Rear-Echelon Maintenance Combined Operations

By the time the Korean War started in 1950, the Air Force had been established as a separate service and the Air Materiel Command had been established. At the same time, evolving technology was changing the logistics landscape. As aircraft became more technically complex after WWII, most maintenance required removing components from the aircraft. These more complex repairs increasingly required special skills, equipment, and technical data from back shops or special installations. To keep pace with these developments, the Air Force replaced the four-echelon system with the three-level maintenance concept in use today. The three-level system consisted of:

1. On-equipment maintenance at the flight line (organizational)
2. Off-equipment maintenance at base shops (intermediate)
3. Off-equipment maintenance at depot facilities (depot).

Even though much maintenance now needed to take place away from aircraft, standard policy still called for it to be decentralized. Yet there was a notable exception to this norm during the Korean War.

[10] Craven and Cate, pp. 369–372.

When favorable conditions during the conflict permitted some combat wings based in Japan to relocate back to Korea, certain Air Force decisionmakers saw an opportunity to try out centralized maintenance. Concerned that maintenance at Korean bases would be vulnerable to disruption while combat was going on, they decided not to bring it all forward to Korea. Instead, they established Rear-Echelon Maintenance Combined Operations (REMCOs) at bases in Japan formerly occupied by the wings now in Korea. The REMCOs performed periodic inspections, field maintenance, engine buildup, and engine overhaul for deployed units.[11] In contrast to the Air Force's standard policy of decentralization, many REMCOs supported more than one combat wing, avoiding duplication of facilities, equipment, and personnel.

REMCOs were very successful. The units supported by REMCOs had better rates of operational readiness, flew more hours, and sustained lower abort and accident rates than units deployed with forward maintenance capabilities. In general, the REMCOs kept aircraft in better condition than their forward-based counterparts.[12] Moreover, when unit aircraft supported by REMCOs were returned to depot, they required significantly fewer hours for reconditioning—2,000 versus 7,500 for a similar group of F-80s.[13]

Despite the objections of many combat commanders who strongly preferred base self-sufficiency, REMCOs became a permanent operation throughout the war.[14] These centralized operations reduced the personnel, equipment, facility, and supply requirements of the combat units, greatly enhancing their ability to move as wartime conditions dictated. The creation of REMCOs enabled the Air Force logistics infrastructure to provide the operational flexibility that fighting forces needed.

---

[11] Futrell, 1961, p. 366.

[12] Nelson, 1953, p. 78.

[13] Moody, 1952.

[14] Spare parts were also centralized at REMCOs, which maintained a 45-day supply level whereas bases were limited to 15-day levels (Futrell, p. 594).

Maintenance Developments After the Korean War

Despite the positive lessons learned from the REMCOs during the Korean War, after the war ended Air Force Headquarters set aside the operational advantages in favor of decentralization. Indeed, the Air Force took a major step toward formalizing a policy of self-sufficiency in 1958, when Headquarters published a directive assigning virtually all personnel, aircraft, equipment, and supplies—everything except aircrews—to the wing's maintenance activity.[15] Although viewed as decentralization given the level of self-sufficiency in those days, in fact maintenance at the unit level was centralized under a single organization. Under this policy, tactical fighter squadrons received efficient and economical logistic support well into the 1960s. Throughout the 1960s, the USAF's primary maintenance objective was, as General Waters stated in his report, "to achieve maximum maintenance at the lowest feasible level." "Toward this end," Waters explained, "action [needed to] be taken to ensure that evacuation of aircraft and components of weapons systems to centralized maintenance areas [was] held to a minimum."[16] Air Force logistics initiatives during this decade focused on developing base capabilities to repair their own aircraft. New budget limitations on the acquisition of spare parts reinforced the motivation behind these efforts, since if a combat unit had only a limited number of serviceable spare parts available, it had to get broken parts back into circulation as quickly as possible. Transporting broken parts to a remote repair location lengthened the pipeline in a way that units could not afford without an ample reserve of spare parts to draw on while broken parts were in transit. It was expected that the bases would repair 85 percent of all reparable components generated by the units flying out of those bases.

The year 1966 marked another major milestone on the road toward full decentralization. Changes to Air Force Manual 26-2 di-

---

[15] Headquarters Air Force, *Maintenance Management*, AFM 66-1. This manual marked the first time that standardized organizational, procedural, and management policies were established for aircraft maintenance. See Tactical Air Command, 1962. The original directive later underwent changes as a result of annual conferences.

[16] Waters, p. 21.

rected that aircraft were to be assigned to fighter squadrons rather than to the wing.[17] The squadrons were, in turn, given an organic capability[18] to remove and replace components, rearm, refuel, and turnaround aircraft. These actions were identified as on-equipment maintenance. Responsibility for performing the bench checks, repair, calibration of components, and Jet Engine Field Maintenance (JEFM) was retained by field maintenance functions at bases. These tasks were categorized as off-equipment maintenance. While on-equipment maintenance could be performed only on aircraft at the site where they were tactically employed, off-equipment maintenance could be performed at the same place as on-equipment maintenance, in a rear-area maintenance activity, or at a depot.

When flying squadrons became responsible for repairing their own aircraft, the pendulum swung fully from centralized or consolidated maintenance at REMCOs to maximum base self-sufficiency. The system was largely problem free until the Tactical Air Command (TAC) began deploying squadron-size units as opposed to entire wings. The most commonly cited complaint was that because the squadron commander and augmentation cells (from the centralized maintenance organization) had not functioned as a squadron-level entity at the squadron's home base, they usually required a transition period after arriving at the employment location to attain the desired efficiency.

The reason base self-sufficiency is important to understanding the evolution of logistical support policies for tactical fighters is that the personnel, equipment, and facility requirements for component bench check and repair are extensive and costly. The heavy equipment also impedes mobility.[19] Even under a policy of base self-sufficiency, it was not difficult to recognize these constraints.

---

[17] These refinements had originally been requested two years earlier by General Hunter Harris, former commander in chief of Pacific Air Forces (PACAF). (Message No. PFCNC 00977 from General Hunter Harris to Lt Gen Thomas Gerrity, November 19, 1964.)

[18] Organic capability refers to unit ownership of resources and materiel to support a particular tasking (e.g., units using their own tools to maintain an engine).

[19] Waters, p. 22.

Project Pacer Sort

On July 7, 1966, the AFLC commander proposed to the Chief of Staff, USAF (CSAF) that a test be conducted to determine if a policy of optimum base self-sufficiency should replace maximum base self-sufficiency. Under an optimum self-sufficiency policy, units would no longer attempt to repair as much as possible at their bases. Instead, they would strive to balance local repair with depot repair. To decide what was better repaired locally and what was better sent to depots, they would evaluate the tradeoffs between such variables as aircraft turnaround time and the reliability and maintainability of repair equipment. Authorized by CSAF, the test was given the code name Pacer Sort.

In introducing the possibility of a balance between base and depot repair, Pacer Sort was the vehicle for a completely new look at logistical support policies for tactical air forces. The test ran for 18 weeks, commencing in February 1967 and ending at the beginning of July. Four squadrons of F-4C aircraft from the 12th Tactical Fighter Wing at Cam Ranh Bay in South Vietnam were divided into a test or TANGO element and a comparative or COCOA element. The Air Force used the TANGO element to assess the effects of increased dependency on AFLC depots in the United States for off-equipment maintenance. The primary objective was to evaluate whether greater dependency degraded the unit's combat capability.[20]

Accounts of the success of this test conflicted. The Pacer Sort report concluded that:

- Both units (TANGO and COCOA) performed equally well
- Reduced self-sufficiency did not degrade the TANGO unit's operational capability
- Considerable quantities of air ground equipment (AGE) were little used during the test

---

[20] Headquarters AFLC, 1967, p. I-II-5-I.

- Direct support by airlift could be just as effective as maximum base self-sufficiency, with certain revisions in maintenance concepts.[21]

However, other analyses rated the test results inconclusive because combat conditions—for example, cannibalization—made it difficult to rigidly enforce test disciplines. Finding that Pacer Sort did not show centralization to offer any clear advantages, the USAF Vice Chief of Staff reaffirmed the need to develop a strong base repair system with existing skills, facilities, and manpower. His directive was included in Project Pacer Sort's final report.[22]

Post-Vietnam Activity

TAC's logistical support policies in the late 1960s and 1970s revolved around the principle of prepositioning: a theater logistical system was fully in place overseas to support forces.[23] This made decentralization a viable and effective option. On the off chance that a crisis arose in a remote geographical area beyond the reach of this in-theater system, where prepositioning was impractical, Air Force planners had a contingency plan. The "Gray Eagle" package was a combined station and housekeeping set that could support tactical contingency operations. This set was kept in a constant state of readiness so that it could deploy with tactical aircraft on first notice.[24] The complete capability to conduct field maintenance could deploy either simultaneously with the tactical squadron or at a later date.[25] Regardless of how and when support was provided, official policy directed that the tactical squadron, with its organizational maintenance, was to maintain its autonomy when deployed.

---

[21] Headquarters AFLC, pp. xv–xxx

[22] Headquarters AFLC, p. I-I-3-I.

[23] Tactical Air Command, 1967, p. 4-1.

[24] Tactical Air Command, 1967, p. 4-1.

[25] Support for field maintenance was to be provided by a host organization supplemented by personnel and equipment from the deployed unit or by another means designated by the theater commander. (Tactical Air Command, 1967, p. 4-3.)

Nevertheless, there was an exception in the Pacific. For Tactical Air Command units deployed to Southeast Asia, PACAF provided logistical support to combat units at Main Support Bases (MSBs) and FOLs.[26] Occupied permanently in peacetime, the MSBs were equipped to support either a wing or several larger operational units. In contrast, FOLs were equipped, manned, and maintained in a reduced operational status during peacetime. In this way, the Air Force could keep resources minimal while ensuring that FOLs would be ready to accept deployed forces on short notice.

Under PACAF's policy, the support assets of a combat squadron deploying to the Pacific could be located at an MSB, FOL, or split between the two. This flexibility enabled PACAF to concentrate resources for off-equipment maintenance on MSBs, which could be located in a nonhostile environment. It also permitted PACAF to reduce the size of the force at FOLs, make them less vulnerable to attack, and make them easier to relocate as operational requirements changed. One can only speculate whether REMCO experiences during the Korean War had affected PACAF's policy formulation in this later period.

A Growing Interest in Centralized Intermediate Maintenance in the 1970s

Although the Air Force's maintenance policy remained predominantly decentralized during the 1970s, there was a growing interest in centralization as an alternative, largely because decentralized maintenance required so much manpower. Aircraft maintenance constituted approximately 25 percent of the Air Force's total manpower, making maintenance personnel a prime area for cuts. All of the commands were searching for ways to reduce total manpower.

In 1973, the commander in chief, U.S. Air Forces in Europe (CINCUSAFE) requested that the USAFE Deputy for Logistics (LG)

---

[26] These policies were specified in *PACAF Deployment Support Manual,* PACAF Manual 400-1, December 1, 1967.

conduct studies to recommend ways of reducing maintenance man-power.[27] "Project Streamline," the first of these analyses, suggested ways to scale back, or even eliminate, small organizations within maintenance and supply, while increasing the workforce's efficiency and productivity. However, the CINC was not impressed with the resulting modest manpower savings.

The Project Streamline team subsequently began to explore other avenues. A literature search led it to the Waters' Air War College report. Compelled by what they read, the team proposed centralized intermediate maintenance for its effects and potential savings for USAFE should one or more centralized intermediate-maintenance facilities replace decentralized intermediate maintenance at all bases in the command. This informal study, "Centralized Intermediate Maintenance Facility," showed greater potential maintenance man-power reductions than the piecemeal reductions proposed under Project Streamline. The project leader briefed the results to General David C. Jones, CINCUSAFE, in June 1974. Interested, General Jones directed that all aspects of a centralized operation be studied carefully—including not just the potential manpower savings but transportation, vulnerability, effects on sortie production, spares availability, and pipeline times.

Before the team could get started, General Jones was transferred to Headquarters to become Chief of Staff of USAF. His successor directed that preparations for a limited test within USAFE be continued. At the request of the then Deputy Chief of Staff of Logistics (USAF/LG), RAND received the briefing in August 1974.[28] Sometime between then and early 1975, in a meeting at RAND, Major Command (MAJCOM) participants agreed on the name "Central-

---

[27] Because of budget shortages, the CINC's objective was not only to cut back the maintenance force but also to support additional aircraft being brought into the Air Force without manpower increases.

[28] This briefing marked RAND's entry into the study of centralized options for maintenance and other logistics operations.

ized Intermediate Repair Facility" (CIRF) as part of an overall "Centralized Intermediate Logistics Concept" (CILC).[29]

USAFE CIRF Test

In the summer of 1975, USAFE conducted a 60-day test of a CIRF at two air bases in the United Kingdom. Royal Air Force (RAF) Bentwaters was designated the CIRF and RAF Woodbridge the FOL. Test planners chose these two bases because their proximity eliminated the need for extensive intratheater transportation. The test was intended to substantiate the savings in personnel and equipment that a CIRF might generate and to look at the CIRF's effects on sortie production. The results were positive, confirming the paper estimates of personnel and equipment savings and showing no CIRF operation limitations as long as there was time-definite delivery of components to the bases being supported by the CIRF.[30]

Maintenance Posture Improvement Program Test

In late 1974, the CSAF authorized a Maintenance Posture Improvement Program (MPIP) for USAFE, PACAF, and the Strategic Air Command (SAC). Testing and implementation of centralized intermediate maintenance became part of the MPIP initiatives.[31] In 1975, PACAF established a trial CIRF for F-4s at Kadena Air Base in Okinawa, Japan. Over a two-year period, this test operation was respon-

---

[29] On his way to take command of PACAF, the USAFE vice-commander sat in on these early briefings. He was interested in the CIRF's potential for reducing forward-based support personnel—particularly because frequent personnel rotations in Korea resulting from short tours of duty were creating high levels of personnel turbulence. The new PACAF commander brought with him a staff summary of the briefings' content, which he intended to give to his Deputy for Logistics in PACAF to review. That Deputy for Logistics was none other than Brigadier General Jack W. Waters.

[30] Following this test, USAFE/LG began preparing for an expanded test, named SALTY SILK, that would involve bases in central Germany. The test plan proposed to establish a CIRF at Spangdahlem Air Base to provide selected maintenance support (primarily avionics and engine) for F-4 aircraft assigned to Spangdahlem, Bitburg, and Hahn Air Bases. However, the test was canceled prior to its planned start because of significant changes in mission design series (MDS) aircraft and mission changes in theater, including the introduction of F-15 aircraft.

[31] Some tests had been launched before the establishment of the MPIP.

sible for most repair support for avionics and engine equipment for aircraft operating out of Kadena, Kunsan, and Osan Air Bases. In 1977, the Kadena CIRF started servicing a fourth unit, an F-4E wing at Clark Air Base in the Philippines.

In June 1977, CINCPACAF concluded that the MPIP test had been successful and the CIRF for the F-4 units would become permanent. The Kadena CIRF operation had achieved one of its objectives: to successfully remove personnel from forward areas. However, the test's key sponsors in PACAF were particularly interested in the effectiveness of centralization as a means of dealing with vulnerability during wartime. For example, would the CIRF help to get personnel and equipment away from forward bases subject to attack? And would it enhance the capability of forces deploying into the theater while reducing initial airlift requirements to forward bases? Along with its successes, the MPIP test pointed to the need to test the CIRF concept under wartime conditions as well as in steady state.

SAC CIRF Test

Between 1975 and 1977, SAC conducted its own test of centralized intermediate maintenance under the auspices of the MPIP.[32] This test, called the Consolidated Repair Concept (CRC), shared the MPIP test's goal of generating personnel reductions. Barksdale Air Force Base in Louisiana was assigned as the CIRF (or CRC) for B-52s and KC-135s at the dual wing at Barksdale. It also supported aircraft from Seymour-Johnson Air Force Base.

The Strategic Air Command's final report indicated that the consolidated repair concept had produced no economies of scale. In fact, the findings showed that the Air Force would need to increase manpower levels to support the concept. Further, to bring sortie production at Seymour-Johnson to adequate pre-test levels, the Air Force would need to increase the on-hand reserves of spare parts necessary to compensate for the pipeline time to the base. The overall conclusion was that a centralized intermediate logistics concept could sup-

---

[32] RAND did not participate in the test or evaluation.

port mission requirements but only at a significant increase in cost. Consequently, after the test ended in September 1977, all units returned to the SAC's standard intermediate-maintenance policy of decentralization at bases.

RAND's CIRF Studies in the 1970s

After initial USAFE testing at RAF Bentwaters/RAF Woodbridge, RAND completed a test study in late 1974 followed by other, related CIRF studies in subsequent years.[33] The RAND team concluded that in addition to generating manpower savings, CIRFs decreased the vulnerability of the maintenance resources collocated with aircraft and offered greater operational flexibility. However, CIRFs increased both the number of serviceable parts that units had to keep in stock and transportation costs. RAND's report pointed out that these advantages and disadvantages were judgmental factors, dependent on the environment under observation and complex wartime variables such as the risk of disruption or destruction of transportation resources.

USAF/LG chartered RAND to conduct a simulation tracking reserve stocks of spare parts at a hypothetical CIRF in Europe supporting ten Main Operating Bases (MOBs) circa 1977. The goal of the simulation was to determine whether the CIRF would necessitate stock increases. The results confirmed that stockage requirements were highly dependent on pipeline times. The RAND team estimated that USAFE would need to generate increased stocks costing up to $57 million for a pipeline time of three to eight days.[34]

WINTEX 77

WINTEX 77 was a Joint Chiefs of Staff (JCS)/NATO wartime simulation exercise of a classified operational plan. During the exercise, analysts identified significant transportation and communica-

---

[33] Berman et al., 1975.

[34] Cohen et al., 1977.

tions shortfalls. The general consensus was that a CIRF structure would have compounded these shortfalls, for two main reasons. First, the additional communications and transportation requirements associated with a "push" system mean that components are delivered not in response to a unit's evolving needs but according to a preplanned supplier schedule. Second, assets need to remain visible at all times, and the exercise demonstrated a lack of visibility. Active USAFE CIRF analysis came to a temporary end. Analysis resumed in July 1977 in response to the MPIPs, headed by the USAF/LG's endorsement of continuing to explore consolidation benefits in USAFE.

USAFE Study

The USAFE study, initiated in September 1977 by the Air Staff (LEY), was conducted by AFLC, Air Force Logistics Management Center (AFLMC), RAND, and HQ USAFE. The objective was to provide insights on how a USAFE CIRF structure might affect combat effectiveness and resource requirements compared with the existing decentralized USAFE support structure. To establish a baseline, the study team formulated a 1982 beddown for F-4, F-15, F-16, and F-111 aircraft. To avoid the complexities of keeping up with out-year changes in the beddown, as well as the need to rework the analyses each time these changes occurred, the study team kept the baseline static.[35]

The study team found insufficient evidence to conclude that centralizing intermediate maintenance within USAFE would increase combat effectiveness. Although the analysis indicated that CIRFs would be affordable and would reduce the vulnerability of intermediate-level maintenance at MOBs by moving maintenance away from the AOR, it also showed the availability of transportation and communications to be quite uncertain. The question mark these uncer-

---

[35] F-111s and F-16s were not thoroughly analyzed because of lack of commonality among F-111 MDS and insufficient spares history for F-16s.

tainties generated eclipsed any advantages the CIRFs could offer.[36] The study team did not anticipate that the transportation and communication issues would be resolved in the near future. For these reasons, the team did not recommend that USAFE commit to the CIRF concept.[37]

CIRF Uses in Operations Desert Shield/Desert Storm

The end of the Cold War resolved many of the issues that had made the prospect of centralizing intermediate maintenance at USAFE bases untenable. Transportation within the European theater and to outlying locations became more certain and bases located in western Europe became significantly more secure. Accordingly, the vulnerability that had played so heavily into decisions not to pursue CIRFs was no longer a factor. When the Persian Gulf War broke out in August 1990 and conditions necessitated that the Air Force seek an alternative to traditional decentralized intermediate maintenance, CIRFs were a viable option.

The beddown for Operations Desert Shield/Desert Storm (DS/DS) split USAF intermediate-level maintenance capability between the AOR in the Middle East and USAFE. While the various

---

[36] In addition, a prospective CIRF at RAF Kimball, a rear location in the United Kingdom that the team had originally thought would be secure, proved to be within range of the Soviet SS-20 missile.

[37] The transportation issues that surfaced during the CIRF studies in the 1970s played an indirect role in leading USAFE to implement what was intended to be an assured and responsive system for distributing needed parts for tactical aircraft during wartime. The European Distribution System (EDS) became operational in March 1985 (see Berman et al., 1981, and Carrillo and Pyles, 1982). A former USAFE/LG commander commented that the EDS could have effectively abetted the CIRF concept. However, EDS was primarily established for lateral support to reduce out-of-service days for USAFE aircraft. The end of the SS-20 and the Soviet threat to Europe made theater CIRFs less of a wartime support issue, and EDS lost its funding and support. Incidentally, when SS-20s were disarmed upon the détente, RAF Kimball was no longer vulnerable to Soviet attack and could have been used as a CIRF. But, ironically, to have been successful, it would have required the phased-out EDS.

commands continued to advocate base self-sufficiency, the AOR could support only a limited number of personnel. The requirements of the crisis necessitated a compromise. By September 1990, the only in-theater avionics intermediate-level maintenance was located at Dhahran, Tabuk, and Thumrait. Much of the other intermediate maintenance was being conducted out of theater:

- Intermediate-level maintenance for the 401st tactical fighter wing was performed at Torrejon, Ramstein, and Hahn Air Bases in Europe.
- An A-10 intermediate-level maintenance capability was planned for King Fahd Air Base, with all other immediate support to come from USAFE locations.
- F-16 units had one Avionics Intermediate Shop per base.
- The F-15E relied on a Mobile Electronic Test Set used to identify bad Line Replaceable Units but not to repair them.
- For Jet Engine Intermediate Maintenance (JEIM), two repair facilities were located in the AOR, with USAFE Queen Bee sites[38] or other external sources providing all other JEIM.
- A "Fast CAL" Precision Measurement Equipment Laboratory (PMEL) was established at Riyadh Air Base and some PMEL support also came from RAF Kemble and Moron Air Base.[39]
- The 7740th Composite Wing's (Proven Force) intermediate-level maintenance was sourced out of USAFE locations for all items except ECM pods. All of this wing's units in the AOR operated with a de facto two-level maintenance operation.
- B-52s were supported out of RAF Fairford and Moron Air Base.[40]

By and large, these centralized facilities performed very well. For example, in the case of the 7740th Composite Wing, the mission ca-

---

[38] A Queen Bee site is essentially another name for a CIRF.

[39] Cohen et al., p. 312.

[40] Cohen et al., p. 334.

pable (MC) rates for units supported outside the theater were comparable to peacetime rates for similar models of aircraft in other units.[41]

The centralized facilities were not completely problem-free. For example, a key problem with JEIM was the lack of an engine management system deployed to the AOR. Without this important command and control (C2) tool, most units deployed without engine records or lost track of engine status. In fact, 11 engines were "lost" because of the lack of a tracking system.

Despite these problems, the centralized operations—CIRFs, Queen Bee sites, and other CIRF-like intermediate-level maintenance centers—provided effective support to Desert Storm units in the AOR. For the first time since the Korean War, centralization proved to be an effective alternative for supporting forward-based units in wartime. In the years following DS/DS, centralization would continue to play a large role in the intermediate-maintenance infrastructure.

---

[41] Cohen et al., p. 326.

CHAPTER THREE

Centralized Maintenance and the AEF Concept

Expeditionary Combat Support

With the Cold War ended, the rapidly changing security environment of the 1990s, and the Air Force's transition to an Air and Space Expeditionary Force, both RAND and the Air Force recognized that the current support system needed improvement to meet operational goals.

One initial goal was for the AEF intended AEFs to deploy from CONUS to any location in the world within 48 hours. RAND analyses[1] examined the operational requirements for an AEF deployment and the support equipment and personnel requirements that the operation would generate. RAND then used logistics process models to compute the requirements for materiel, equipment, and people to establish and operate the process; RAND also evaluated alternative infrastructure options in providing these requirements.[2]

Based on these analyses, it became clear that the 48-hour timeline could not be met solely with deployments from CONUS to bare bases. RAND instead proposed an Agile Combat Support/

---

[1] See, for example, Tripp et al., 1999; Galway et al., 2000; and Tripp et al., 2000.

[2] For a comprehensive review of RAND ACS research, see Rainey et al., 2003.

mobility system[3] with the flexibility to respond to a variety of scenarios. RAND's ACS vision had five components: FOLs, FSLs, CSLs, transportation, and CSC2. The specific configuration of these components depends on numerous factors and will evolve as operational needs change.

The Air Force has developed the ACS concept and implemented RAND's FOL/FSL/CSL vision in long-range plans, wargames, and, eventually, in real-world operations. Figure 3.1 presents a timeline of RAND analyses regarding AEF deployments and the Air Force actions influenced by their results.

RAND has also developed the ACS concept, particularly the use of FSLs for intermediate maintenance. The immediate needs of flightline maintenance generally require that some maintenance capability be deployed to FOLs, and the diversity and uncertainty of

Figure 3.1
Timeline of RAND and Air Force Development of the AEF Concept

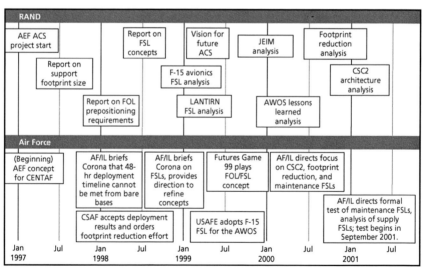

RAND MG151-3.1

_____

[3] Hereafter referred to as the ACS system.

needs for depot-level maintenance require that some repair capability be maintained in the CONUS. However, as standing repair organizations located near, but not necessarily in, the theater of operations, FSLs offer the potential to reduce the footprint as units deploy to FOLs, as well as offering economies of scale by consolidating repair of multiple units' commodities to a single location.

We evaluated the FOL/FSL/CSL concept in terms of the repair resources it required and the ability of centralized intermediate maintenance to support potential contingency scenarios. We examined maintenance support concepts for F-15 avionics, LANTIRN pods (see Figure 3.2) and jet engines (see Figure 3.3), and, more broadly, analyzed the implementation of maintenance FSLs, including:

- A study of several potential FSL locations and their potential benefits and vulnerabilities

Figure 3.2
LANTIRN Testing

RAND *MG151-3.2*

Figure 3.3
Jet Engine Intermediate-Maintenance Shop

RAND *MG151–3.3*

- An analysis of deployment footprint, how it is measured, and how it might be reduced
- A look at the Air Force's CSC2 architecture and how it might affect FSL implementation.

Furthermore, we examined the implementation of maintenance FSLs in wargames and in the Air War Over Serbia to determine how performance of these facilities could be improved.

Maintenance FSL Options by Commodity

Traditionally, intermediate-maintenance operations have been deployed with combat units to their FOLs. The goal of the RAND commodity studies, conducted between 1998 and 2000, was to evaluate alternative options to this decentralized, deployed maintenance support. We approached the analysis with a series of quantitative models. Whereas the ideal configurations of support locations always depend on tradeoffs between a unit's operational needs and the availability of resources, in each case studied we found that a network that used FSLs and CSLs, with the proper transportation and C2 support, had the potential to improve performance over the traditional system. These options reduced deployment footprint, which in turn reduced the time to operational readiness. They also used maintenance facilities to support a number of operating locations, not only the location in which they are established. This enabled greater operational flexibility, key to the success of the AEF.

F-15 Avionics[4]

The traditional decentralized system for avionics repair has presented several challenges in the expeditionary environment. To meet sortie requirements for the wide range of deployments faced today, deploying the avionics intermediate shop (AIS) to FOLs requires more highly skilled personnel than are currently available in the Air Force. As a result, these personnel are likely to face continued frequent deployments and are unable to provide junior technicians with the guidance they need, contributing to retention problems among avionics technicians. Furthermore, under current doctrine, for small-scale contingencies avionics testers are deployed as a single set, or "string": Each deploying unit brings with it only one set of test equipment. This places deployed units at risk, because a single tester failure would leave a unit without any repair capability until the tester is repaired.

We compared the performance of four options—the current decentralized, deployed AIS network and three alternatives:

---

[4] For more information on F-15 avionics maintenance see Peltz et al., 2000.

- *Decentralized–deployed* [5] (base case). Each F-15 squadron has its own avionics repair capacity that deploys with it to FOLs.
- *Decentralized–no deployment.* Each F-15 squadron uses an AIS that belongs to its wing, located at its wing's home base in the United States, that distributes needed avionics components to the squadron when it is deployed.
- *CONUS support locations.* All F-15 squadrons receive needed avionics components through distribution networks extending from centralized intermediate repair locations in the United States.
- *CONUS support location–forward support location.* All F-15 squadrons active in a particular region of the world receive needed avionics components from an avionics intermediate shop prepositioned at an FSL in that region and linked to a central U.S.-based repair location.

We evaluated each of these alternatives on the criteria of spin-up time, cost, deployment footprint, operational risk, operational flexibility, and degree of personnel stability likely to result. We reached the following conclusions:

- The decentralized–deployed option offers operational flexibility in that all avionics intermediate shops are self-sufficient and do not require the Air Force to set up a distribution pipeline to move components between repair and forward locations. This self-sufficiency significantly reduces operational risk. However, this option increases deployment footprint, places a strain on personnel, and raises the issue of "single-string risks" when only one tester is deployed to each FOL.
- The three alternatives in which the AIS is not deployed to the FOLs also offer operational flexibility but in a different context.

---

[5] We label each alternative in terms of "peacetime repair–wartime repair." For example, the decentralized–deployed case implies a decentralized mode of repair during peacetime (and for non-engaged forces) at home units and deployed maintenance shops at the forward operating locations.

Although they rely heavily on the distribution pipeline for sustainment, without heavy maintenance equipment to move, combat forces can be ready for operations rapidly.

- Centralized repair of avionics components in the third and fourth options provides levels of support similar to existing operations. The associated reduction in personnel turbulence, unit deployment footprint, and "single-string risks" associated with the decentralized deployed system, as well as the shorter pipeline for FSLs as compared to CSLs, provide additional advantages for the CSL-FSL option.

In summary, a network of FSLs and a CSL for avionics repair is cost competitive with the base case and addresses each of its disadvantages. Moderate personnel deployment to nonhostile locations eliminates equipment deployment to the AOR and the risks associated with this movement. Although these benefits are somewhat offset by the need to quickly establish effective intratheater distribution and the risk associated with losing transportation capability, the AEF emphasis on quick deployment and employment makes the CSL-FSL option a favorable one.

LANTIRN Pods[6]

In our LANTIRN analysis, we evaluated six intermediate-maintenance infrastructures (the traditional decentralized structure, and five alternatives involving varying degrees of centralization), defined by the number of facilities required and how test equipment, personnel, and spares were distributed among these locations.

- *Decentralized–deployed* (base case). Repair capability deploys with the combat units to the FOLs.
- *Complete centralization*. All intermediate maintenance consolidated at a single CSL.
- *One CSL–Two FSLs*. FSLs are in USAFE and PACAF to support contingencies in Southwest Asia and Northeast Asia, and a CSL

---

[6] For a detailed LANTIRN analysis, see Feinberg et al., 2001.

meets the peacetime demands of all CONUS-based aircraft. During a contingency, as CONUS units are deployed overseas, CSL personnel could be shifted to FSLs to support them.

- *Two CSLs–Two FSLs.* FSLs are in USAFE and PACAF; two facilities are in CONUS.
- *Two CSLs.* Identical in concept to the complete centralization option, this alternative may offer strategic advantages in supporting multiple contingencies.
- *Mixed–virtual alternative.* Two CSLs are supplied with resources for three locations, one in CONUS and two outside of CONUS, with CSL capacity deployed to other locations as combat units deploy for a contingency.

We modeled the performance of each of these options in a two-MRC (major regional conflict) scenario, which involved successive contingencies in separate parts of the world. This scenario was rigorous enough that any infrastructure that could generate enough resources to satisfy its demands would also be able to satisfy less-demanding missions. The alternatives were then analyzed in connection with AEF objectives, including LANTIRN availability, transportation requirements, and the reduction of footprint, risk, and costs.

We reached the following conclusions:

- Options using FSLs require fewer test sets and fewer highly skilled personnel than the decentralized-deployed maintenance option. These options also have a much lower deployment footprint than deploying maintenance to the FOLs. The footprint savings also reduces the need for strategic airlift at the beginning of a deployment.
- All of the centralized maintenance options, both those using CSLs alone and those integrating CSLs and FSLs, reduce the risk of "single-string" failures, because centralized facilities are resourced with enough test equipment that one failure would not halt all operations. These options also eliminate the need to

transport repair equipment to support various contingencies. Because test equipment transport and setup times can be long, and equipment readiness is unpredictable once in theater, the CSL-FSL options offer a more stable support system.

- Because FSLs are removed from the theater of operations, personnel and support equipment face lower risks in the infrastructures that include FSLs. Although larger, centralized operations may be more vulnerable to attack, proper preparation and communications design can help to alleviate these threats.

- The decentralized repair structure requires a greater investment in support equipment, increasing the financial burden to the Air Force. The options using FSLs generally have higher annual transportation costs but lower annual labor costs. The total recurring peacetime costs, which outweigh the initial investment costs, are essentially equivalent.

- As in the F-15 avionics analysis, the advantages of centralized LANTIRN maintenance are sensitive to the availability and effectiveness of transportation. If transportation is not readily available, the options using FSLs lose their efficiency, and base self-sufficiency becomes a more desired quality.

- In summary, the centralized maintenance structure introduces new risks to the Air Force and requires a new set of support processes. For successful implementation of centralized maintenance, unit commanders would need to relinquish some of their control over resources and must communicate closely with support centers and other bases serviced by the same facility. Performance metrics might also need to be changed to reflect the system's focus on warfighter readiness. However, the risks introduced by FSLs are offset by the economies of scale they provide and the reduction of "single-string" risks. Furthermore, the flexibility and footprint reduction provided by centralized maintenance offer distinct advantages in the current environment.

Jet Engine Intermediate Maintenance[7]

The Air Force's JEIM needs have posed particular challenges in the expeditionary environment. Engines are large, heavy, and require cumbersome maintenance equipment. Furthermore, once repaired, engines are attached to cement test cells, and tested at full power. These test cells need approximately 30 days to be set up and for the concrete to harden. Standing FSLs for JEIM were considered to reduce the deployment footprint and setup time required for engine maintenance. In this analysis, we simulated the performance of the following centralized and decentralized maintenance options in supporting forces deployed to a notional 100-day MRC:

- *Decentralized–deployed* (base case). JEIM support is decentralized to each base in peacetime; part of each base's JEIM deploys with the aircraft to the FOL in war.
- *Decentralized–no deployment.* JEIM support is decentralized to each base in peacetime; during war, each base JEIM supports its own deployed unit.
- *Decentralized–FSL.* JEIM support is decentralized to each base in peacetime; during war, a single JEIM is set up in the theater to support all deployed units with a given type of engine.
- *CSL–FSL.* All units are supported in peacetime by a single centralized JEIM facility in CONUS; personnel from the CSL deploy to a theater FSL to support deployed units in war. In the theater, this option's performance is identical to the previous one.
- *CSLs.* All units are supported in peacetime or during war by a single centralized JEIM facility in CONUS.

We evaluated the performance of each of these alternatives for three different engines: the F100-220, the F100-229, and the TF-34. We determined the personnel and equipment levels required at each repair facility to ensure that no required wartime sorties were missed,

---

[7] For a detailed analysis of jet engine maintenance options see Amouzegar et al., 2001.

and then compared the spares levels that each alternative allowed combat units to maintain over the course of our notional major conflict. Finally, we examined the personnel and transportation requirements for each maintenance alternative, to see how maintenance performance would be affected by a gain or loss of resources.

We reached the following major conclusions:

- For support of a fast-breaking major conflict, the option of deploying the JEIM to the FOL is too slow to provide adequate support with acceptable spares levels. Because of the Air Force's planned deployment schedule and the time required to assemble the engine test cell, deployed JEIM takes 60 days to reach complete functionality. In these 60 days, based on expected engine failure rates, this alternative requires a large inventory of spares to avoid a buildup of aircraft without engines.
- For the F100-220 and F100-229, locating the JEIM facility at an FSL is the best alternative. As standing organizations, FSLs can provide repair support as soon as a new conflict warrants. Furthermore, FSLs located near the theater of operations allow a shorter pipeline than repair consolidated in CONUS. However, this option requires dependable intratheater transportation.
- For the TF-34, either an FSL or CSL provides acceptable performance. The TF-34 has a lower removal rate than the F-100 series, and units therefore expect fewer planes to be without engines at any given time. As a result, there is less of a need for spare parts, and these aircraft can tolerate longer repair cycle times, from either FSLs or CSLs, because they do not need to move parts as frequently.
- In peacetime, centralizing repair for small F100-220 bases in CONUS could provide some resource savings.
- For each engine type, centralized alternatives require dedicated and responsive transportation. Any deviation from the times assumed in our modeling can significantly affect their performance. For example, we assumed that transportation to and from the FSL is two to four days. Even a small increase causes a loss in combat sorties.

In summary, for the engine types analyzed in this study, centralized intermediate repair provides several advantages over the current decentralized-deployed repair structure, such as the immediate availability of repair capability, reduced resource requirements, and reduced deployment footprint. In contrast, the time required to deploy and establish JEIM capability makes the traditional structure undesirable in the expeditionary environment.

However, there are a number of qualitative issues that must be addressed in FSL implementation. FSL support is very sensitive to the availability and performance of transportation. Without efficient transportation, units are unable to transfer engines to and from repair as needed. Furthermore, consolidating maintenance raises issues of control of JEIM resources supporting multiple bases. Finally, issues remain with the transition to wartime if a decentralized structure is retained for peacetime but FSL support is planned for a conflict.

Summary: Commodity Studies

In each of these commodity studies, centralized intermediate maintenance has the potential to substitute for forward-deployed repair and can provide the Air Force with considerable benefits toward AEF objectives. Collocation of intermediate-level maintenance personnel and equipment creates economies of scale and reduces the amount of equipment and personnel required to meet operational requirements. Furthermore, by developing centralized facilities with a larger collection of repair resources and personnel with varying skill levels, centralized facilities can increase the availability and reliability of equipment and increase opportunities for technical training of junior staff.

These analyses also suggest that in order to best take advantage of the consolidated intermediate repair structure, supporting procedures must be in place. Performance of FSLs and CSLs is heavily dependent on effective C2 and intratheater distribution, each of which needs system-wide improvements. The Air Force will also need to modify its organizational structure and measures of effectiveness to fit the new repair structure. The results discussed in this chapter are summarized in Table 3.1.

Table 3.1
Summary of Results

Commodity	Number of FSLs	Number of CSLs	Resupply Time (Days)	Comments
F-15 avionics	3–4	1	3–7	Number of facilities reflects tradeoff between increasing transportation time and spares requirements
LANTIRN	2	2	2–4	Number of facilities bracketed by available repair equipment, number of pods, and transportation times
Engines	3–5	3	4–6	Main drivers are number of spare engines and start-up time
ECM pods	2–3	1	2–4	Very sensitive to removal rate/failure mode

Location Selection for Maintenance FSLs [8]

In addition to transportation availability and C2 performance, the success of centralized intermediate maintenance depends on where FSL facilities are situated. Although FSLs must be close enough to the theater of operations to ensure rapid transportation to and from the FOLs, these needs must be balanced with the risk that might be incurred by placing an FSL within enemy reach. Decisions about where to locate FSLs should also consider obstacles that could impede access to the sites. In some cases, access to a potential FSL might be limited because in the future a permanent U.S. presence may not be welcome. In other cases, the threat of terrorism may reduce the reliability of access. In regions of political instability, access may also be limited by political conflict or changes in government.

---

[8] Potential FSL locations are analyzed in LaTourrette et al., 2003. (The report is not available for public release.)

Potential FSL sites must be evaluated to determine their infrastructure and operating requirements. Certain sites may require the Air Force to augment the existing infrastructure by constructing warehouse and shop space or converting existing warehouse space to shop space. These costs could vary widely, depending on the capabilities of the proposed sites and the requirements of the conflicts being prepared for. The site evaluations must also consider that operating requirements for maintenance facilities are likely to change as they are moved from FOLs to FSLs. A network of FSLs would entail substantial redistribution of transportation and personnel resources from the current decentralized system. Intratheater transportation would increase, whereas intertheater deployment transport would be reduced. These changes may make some sites more or less appropriate as FSLs than they might otherwise have been.

While some of the traits desired in FSLs, such as proximity to FOLs and distance from enemy operations, are inherently at odds with each other, they must all be considered in establishing centralized intermediate repair operations. Tradeoffs can then be established according to strategic priorities, so that FSLs can most effectively support expeditionary operations.

Forward Support Locations in the Air War Over Serbia

In May 1998, USAF/IL briefed the FSL concept at the CORONA meeting. On the basis of the potential deployment reductions provided by FSLs, the Air Force decided to refine these new combat support concepts for implementation. In 1999, USAFE/LG supported a formal test of FSLs for repair of LANTIRN pods and F-15 avionics. When plans for this test were interrupted by the Air War Over Serbia, USAFE implemented maintenance FSLs in support of the war.

Three existing USAFE repair facilities—RAF Lakenheath, Aviano Air Base, and Spangdahlem Air Base—had already been operating informally as FSLs prior to the outset of the AWOS. During the conflict, the Air Force formally designated them as CIRFs. Additionally, CIRF operations at RAF Mildenhall were developed during the conflict, primarily supporting KC-135 Isochronal (ISO) and refueling-boom maintenance.

The CIRFs used in support of Joint Task Force Noble Anvil provided several benefits over the traditional decentralized-deployed maintenance structure. Because CIRFs were developed to support repair at a variety of locations, they enabled greater operational flexibility. They also reduced deployment footprints for intermediate-level maintenance by about two-thirds in terms of test equipment and personnel. The established intermediate-level maintenance infrastructure permitted almost instantaneous spin-up of repair operations.

However, the USAFE combat support (CS) structure had not been set up to accommodate the CIRF concept.[9] For example, planning and control of the Theater Distribution System (TDS) were slow to evolve. Early in the operation, prompted by the need for express transportation in support of the CIRF concept, USAFE/LG requested a change in EUCOM's (European Command's) distribution policies. EUCOM requirements were traditionally presented in terms of volume (for example, short tons to be moved per day), whereas USAFE was most concerned with rapid and time-definite distribution of both serviceable and unserviceable materiel. The difference in distribution policies meant that the Air Force's initial metrics did not provide an adequate view of how transportation performance would affect operational readiness.

Furthermore, the CSC2 network supporting CIRF operations had several issues. For instance, the organizational structure shifted from its doctrinal form, in which the Numbered Air Force (NAF) performed CS planning, execution, and control functions, to one in which the USAFE/LG staff performed these functions. The USAFE/LG staff was not trained for these responsibilities. Its members were organized into "control cells" to manage the elements of the CS system, and each operated without established policy guidelines to govern their actions. The control cells' use of innovative reporting

---

[9] Feinberg et al., 2002.

and control processes was critical to the Air Force's ability to support escalating operations.

Although the ad hoc implementation of the CIRF concept presented challenges, the benefits of the CIRFs, most notably their ability to instantaneously begin repair operations at a reduced footprint, were undeniable. These positive results compelled the Air Force to further examine CIRF operations and the ACS concepts surrounding them.

Footprint Configuration Analysis

The traditional concept of footprint was conceptually simple: it was measured in terms of the mass of materiel and the number of people to be moved. To more easily monitor deployment footprint and its reduction, we presented a capability-based concept of footprint configuration,[10] in which the materiel and personnel required for any support process are divided into five parts:

- *Initial operating requirements (IORs)*: materiel and personnel needed at the FOL to initiate operations, or give the base Initial Operating Capability (IOC).
- *Full operating requirements (FORs)*: materiel and personnel needed at the FOL to sustain operations and to bring the base to full operating capability (FOC).
- *On-call*: materiel and personnel needed at the FOL but only in specific circumstances.
- *FSL*: materiel and personnel not necessarily required to be at the FOL. These resources can be provided at FSLs or elsewhere in the theater.
- *CSL*: materiel and personnel that are not necessarily needed at the FOL or in theater but can be provided from the CONUS.

---

[10] Galway et al., 2003.

This new concept of footprint defined deployment requirements in terms of the resources needed to provide specific operating capabilities, instead of simply the physical mass of items to be moved over the course of a deployment. Accordingly, the RAND team proposed that the time and transportation required to move both the IOR and FOR would serve as the primary metrics for assessing footprint configurations. To keep these metrics low, planners could then make tradeoffs in several other key areas, such as materiel mass, flexibility, and risk.

To ensure that future deployment planning reflects this new capability-based concept of footprint, RAND recommended that the Air Force:

- Restructure support processes to emphasize footprint reconfiguration.
- Develop a comprehensive, parameterized list of unit type codes (UTCs) needed to deploy a given force capability to a base with a specified infrastructure.
- Exercise more centralized control of UTC development to ensure that there is a system view of UTC modifications.
- Track changes in deployment speed and other major metrics for selected combinations of force packages and base infrastructure, to evaluate progress.
- Set up a system to aggregate the force/base evaluations to theater level for current war plans. This system should also provide strategic support planning for proposed plans.
- Develop tools to help decisionmakers evaluate and select among alternative footprint configurations.

C2 Analysis

The AWOS highlighted the importance of effective C2 in Air Force operations. In the conflict, disconnects between operational planners and support planners led to delays in operations, and the lack of a feedback system made it difficult for the Air Force to take corrective actions when operations were not going as planned. These disconnects were particularly notable in the implementation of CIRFs, when logistics organizations had difficulty responding to the demands of centralized maintenance. USAFE had difficulty communicating its transportation needs to EUCOM, and therefore did not always have transportation available when needed. This caused USAFE difficulties in the support of remote maintenance operations.

Because these C2 issues are critical to all aspects of CS operations, the Air Force asked RAND to standardize the Air Force's CSC2 infrastructure in an architecture that could be applied to operations worldwide, and to propose modifications as appropriate. In our analysis, we presented concepts for guiding the development of the architecture for the AEF.[11] Our analysis of the Air Force's CS execution planning and control process revealed important shortfalls in the *AS-IS* architecture. We grouped these shortfalls into four categories:

- Poor integration of CS input into operational planning
- Absence of resource allocation/prioritization mechanisms across competing theaters
- Poor coordination of Air Force activities with the joint-service community
- Absence of feedback loops and ability to reconfigure the CS infrastructure dynamically.

To address these concerns, we proposed a *TO-BE* combat support execution planning and control architecture that would enable the Air Force to meet its AEF operational goals. The architecture has several elements that would enable the CS community to quickly estimate support requirements for force package options and assess the feasibility of operational and support plans. Clearly defined processes that integrate support and operational needs would permit quick determination of beddown needs and capabilities, facilitate rapid Time

---

[11] Leftwich et al., 2002.

Phased Force and Deployment Data (TPFDD) development, and support development and configuration of a theater distribution network to meet employment timelines and resupply needs. These processes will enable improved coordination between the operational and CS communities, across theaters, and between the Air Force and the joint-service community. The *TO-BE* architecture also uses feedback loops to measure actual performance against plans and indicate when CS performance deviates from desired states. Such links between planning and execution help planners determine the operational impacts of scarce resource allocation and facilitate development of resupply plans and the implementation of "get-well" plans. This will enable the Air Force to reconfigure its CS infrastructure as operations progress.

For the Air Force CS community to move from its *AS-IS* architecture to the proposed *TO-BE* concept, we recommended several steps.

- Summarize and clarify Air Force CS doctrine and policy; articulate the functions of the CSC2 architecture
- Create standing CS organizations to reduce the turbulence associated with the transition from supporting one contingency to another
- Train operations and CS personnel about each other's C2 roles, responsibilities, and methods so that each group can incorporate the other's needs into their plans
- Field appropriate information system and decision-support tools to translate CS resource levels and processes into operational capabilities or effects.

Each of these changes will lay a foundation with which the Air Force can improve its CS system and move toward the AEF objectives. Better CSC2 will allow for centralization of decisionmaking and other support activities, more comprehensive performance metrics, and a better understanding of ongoing operations to enable the implementation and ongoing operation of CIRFs and other support facilities.

Summary: Maintenance FSLs and the AEF

Since the inception of the AEF concept, each of the RAND analyses of intermediate-maintenance concepts has shown that a network of centralized intermediate repair facilities (most using a combination of FSLs and CSLs) has the potential to reduce deployment footprint, thereby improving speed of deployment while providing support comparable to that of the traditional decentralized-deployed maintenance structure. They also enable greater operational flexibility, because maintenance FSLs are intended to support a range of operating locations and adapt to changing conditions. However, our analyses also revealed that the success of maintenance FSLs is dependent on reliable C2 and intratheater transportation, and that each of these networks is still in need of improvement.

Based at least in part on these findings, on CIRF performance in the AWOS, and a number of other factors, the Air Force developed a formal test of the centralized intermediate-maintenance concept. The AF/IL CIRF test, conducted between September 2001 and February 2002, was meant to determine the level of support resources necessary to facilitate maintenance operations.

CHAPTER FOUR

Maintenance FSL Operations: The CIRF Test

Background

The USAFE/LG, partly based on RAND centralized intermediate-maintenance and CIRF-based studies, was moving toward conducting a formal test of overseas CIRFs when war erupted in Serbia in 1999. The resulting Air Force operations interrupted plans for an official test. Instead, the Air Force implemented overseas CIRFs (FSLs) during the AWOS on an ad hoc basis.

The Air Force's experiences with overseas CIRFs during this conflict demonstrated that centralized intermediate maintenance could successfully support a contingency under wartime conditions. However, problems associated with implementation underscored the need for a formal test. For example, augmentation of overseas facilities with personnel and equipment from CONUS and other processes needed to be studied more thoroughly and better defined. In the years following the war, the USAFE/LG who had originally advocated for a test moved to a position in AF/ILM. In this capacity, she was able to recommend a test of the CIRF concept that would have implications for the entire Air Force rather than only USAFE. As a result, in November 2000, AF/IL directed a formal test of maintenance FSLs, commonly referred to as the CIRF test.

The CIRF Concept of Operations (CONOPS) identified four scenarios that CIRFs could potentially support:

- **Peacetime**: CIRFs provide CONUS and outside of CONUS (OCONUS) regional intermediate repair to support normal flying training operations (e.g., Engine Regional Repair Centers at Dyess, Shaw, and Misawa Air Bases).
- **Steady-state**: CIRFs provide regional intermediate repair to support three-month AEF rotations to Operations Northern and Southern Watch (ONW/OSW). Because AEF rotations are only three months long, and the manpower augmentation for CIRFs is therefore only temporary, CIRFs provide only minor engine maintenance to supported units.
- **Contingency**: CIRFs provide regional intermediate repair to support small-scale rapid-response deployments to multiple global locations (e.g., support given during Operation Allied Force).
- **Major Regional Conflict**: CIRFs provide regional intermediate repair to support tasked OPLAN operations.

The test was intended to examine CIRF operations in one of these scenarios: steady-state operations. It measured and evaluated CIRF support for units deployed during consecutive AEF rotations to ONW/OSW. The units in the test flew out of Southwest Asia (SWA) bases and used the CIRFs at RAF Lakenheath, Spangdahlem Air Base, and Aviano Air Base (pictured in Figure 4.1), the same facilities that had been used in AWOS. The objective of the CIRF test was to determine the transportation, repair, and supply requirements for sustaining operations.

The operational concept of the CIRF test was a microcosm of RAND's global ACS vision, with support activities performed outside the AOR to reduce deployment footprint but connected to FOLs via a transportation and C2 network. However, the AF/IL test deviated from the RAND concept in two notable ways. First, the test included only overseas CIRFs, rather than the FSL/CSL vision proposed by RAND. The test maintained base-level support in CONUS and deployed intermediate-repair capability to the CIRFs as units deployed to the theater.

Figure 4.1
CIRF Test Operational Environment

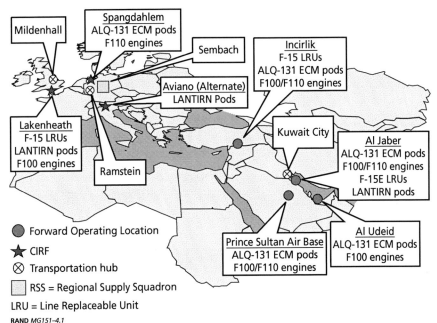

Second, the RAND ACS network envisioned that the Air Force would centralize ownership of CIRF commodities and centrally fund their repair, so that newly serviceable engines and pods could be allocated to those units with the most pressing operational needs without having to complete all of the paperwork normally involved in transferring items from one unit to another. While the CIRF test utilized a "remove-and-replace" concept for F-15 LRUs, it maintained a "repair-and-return" policy for engines and pods.

In the remainder of this chapter, we discuss the Air Force's implementation of the test and the test results.[1]

---

[1] See Headquarters Air Force/ILMM, June 2002, for more information.

CIRF Test Plan

The Air Force took a thorough, end-to-end view of the CIRF test, creating a well-defined concept of operations and a detailed test plan that contained guidelines for CIRF organization and operations. It established planning factors for personnel and support equipment to guide deployment. These factors, based on the total number of unit-deployed aircraft or pods, identified the corresponding personnel and support equipment required for the deploying unit. Specific skill level and work schedule requirements were left to be coordinated between the CIRF and the deploying units. The test plan also contained five criteria for measuring performance that examined the CIRF's ability to support operations, the effectiveness of CIRF decisionmaking, and the financial, equipment, and personnel resources required.[2]

In developing the plan, the CIRF test planners drew upon several of RAND's earlier recommendations.[3] One of these recommendations had been to establish a single organization in charge of allocation and decisionmaking for all CIRF operations. In the CIRF test, planners assigned these responsibilities to the USAFE Regional Supply Squadron (USAFE/RSS). The USAFE/RSS combines two types of C2 responsibilities: supply and transportation.

Supply Responsibilities	Transportation Responsibilities
• Mission capability (MICAP) management	• Shipment tracing and tracking
• Stock control	• Source selection
• Stock fund management	• Traffic management research

---

[2] Headquarters Air Force/ILMM, 2002.

[3] At the time of the CIRF test, our work on CSC2 architecture had been briefed throughout the Air Force, although it was not yet published, and several of the RAND recommendations were incorporated into the test plan. The CSC2 recommendations were eventually published in Leftwich et al., 2002.

The organizational structure of the USAFE/RSS is shown in Figure 4.2.

The RSS is capable of interfacing with the maintainers at the CIRF, providing combatant commanders with operational materiel distribution C2, regional weapon system support, and a comprehensive picture of the CIRF's needs. Because all repair actions in the test were to take place at USAFE CIRFs, AF/ILM-T concluded that the USAFE/RSS would be able to coordinate with the CIRFs most easily. Also, because the USAFE/RSS was organized as a cross-functional logistics team, AF/ILM reasoned that it would be best able to prioritize, induct, and distribute CIRF assets.

The RSS was also responsible for assessing the availability of weapon systems and the condition of deployed units. These assessments are essential to CIRF operations because they provide capability-based measures of CIRF repair effectiveness. Because they require global visibility and coordination, they were conducted during the CIRF test at both the USAFE/RSS and the Air Combat Command (ACC)/RSS.

The CIRF test plan also drew from RAND's recommendation to define decision rules before executing a plan. The CIRF CONOPS clearly stated that engine CIRFs would be capable of performing

Figure 4.2
USAFE/RSS Organizational Structure

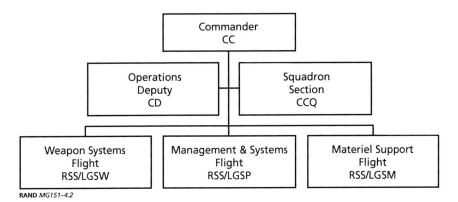

RAND MG151–4.2

either minor or major intermediate maintenance, but that they would perform only minor maintenance for the steady-state operations during the test. They would leave the major maintenance to home units in most circumstances. The CONOPS also defined how items would be inducted and distributed on a repair-and-return basis, in keeping with the unit-ownership policy used during the test.

Finally, the CIRF test plan built upon the RAND vision of a feedback loop, which compares actual support performance with expected performance, warns of potential operational impacts, and tells support planners when to modify either the support or operational plans to accommodate logistics constraints. In accordance with this vision, CIRF personnel developed an information system known as the CIRF toolkit to provide a common operating picture to all those involved with CIRF operations. The CIRF toolkit was a set of tools hosted on the Air Force portal to provide the status of aircraft, engines, pods, and F-15 avionics Line Replaceable Units (LRUs).[4] The toolkit also contained a database to track transportation pipeline segments so that personnel could compare actual performance against planned values.[5] This system leveraged the efforts of the ongoing Strategic Defense Management Initiative[6] to ensure adequate distribution support.

---

[4] The legacy source systems involved were Core Automated Maintenance System (CAMS), Comprehensive Engine Management System (CEMS), Reliability, Availability, and Maintainability database for electronic warfare pods (RAMPOD), and Standard Base Supply system (SBSS), respectively. The primary users were a cell in the USAFE/RSS at Sembach Air Base, and the Headquarters Air Force/ILMM CIRF action officers.

[5] The communication channels were the World Wide Web, telephone, and e-mails. Although these channels of communication were adequate, the logistics processes displayed in the CIRF toolkit required additional manual intervention to provide Total Asset Visibility (TAV) for logistics C2.

[6] The Strategic Distribution Management Initiative (SDMI), now adopted as common practice and referred to solely as Strategic Distribution (SD), was developed to improve transportation performance and time-definite delivery.

The CIRF test involved five wing-level USAFE work centers (as CIRFs) to support AEF deployed units for intermediate repair requirements across engines, pods, and F-15 avionics LRUs.[7] In October 2001, the United States launched Operation Enduring Freedom (OEF), an operation that shared many of the combat and support resources used in ONW/OSW. Engines and pods that failed during OEF were also repaired at the USAFE CIRFs being tested. Although this was not part of the initial plan, it permitted the Air Force to observe CIRF operations under wartime conditions. Data were collected on the performance of the five CIRF work centers at two locations: the 48th Component Repair Squadron (CRS) at RAF Lakenheath and the 52nd CRS at Spangdahlem Air Base. Operation Enduring Freedom and the additional demand that it generated forced the CIRF operations to deviate from the test plan. For example, repair of LANTIRN pods was not planned to begin until AEF 9/10. However, additional pods generated during OEF caused such a backlog at the RAF Lakenheath CIRF that another CIRF, the 31st CRS at Aviano Air Base, was established to repair the additional pods (see Table 4.1).

Table 4.1
CIRF Operation

CIRF Location	CIRF Type	Forward Operating Location
48th CRS at Lakenheath	F-15 avionics LANTIRN F100-PW engines	Incirlik, Al Jaber, Al Udeid, Prince Sultan Air Base
52nd CRS at Spangdahlem	ECM pods F110-GE engines	Incirlik, Al Jaber, Al Udeid, Prince Sultan Air Base
31st CRS at Aviano	LANTRIN pods	Al Jaber

---

[7] Headquarters Air Force/ILMM, 2002.

Results

The CIRFs supported 154 deployed aircraft, including F-15s and F-16s; they repaired 38 engines, 67 ECM pods, 24 LANTIRN pods, and 170 F-15 avionics LRUs.

Operational Achievements

The CIRF test demonstrated that centralized intermediate maintenance was capable of supporting steady-state operations and reducing the associated personnel and equipment footprint. Further analysis showed that CIRFs had the potential to achieve an even greater savings in support of an MRC. The steady-state logistics footprint savings for ECM pods and the expected MRC savings for avionics components, LANTIRN pods, and JEIM are illustrated in Figures 4.3 and 4.4.

The manpower requirements detailed here corresponded closely to those in the test plan. Table 4.2 details the actual manpower requirements compared to expectations.

Figure 4.3
Personnel/Support Equipment Deployment Savings, Steady-State

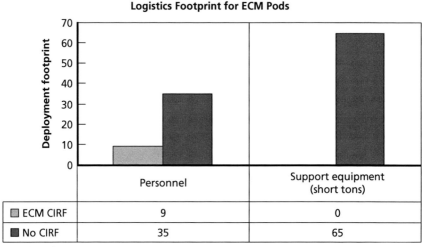

	Personnel	Support equipment (short tons)
ECM CIRF	9	0
No CIRF	35	65

RAND *MG151–4.3*

Figure 4.4
Personnel/Support Equipment Deployment Savings, MRC Projection

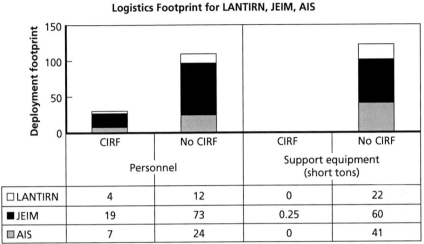

Logistics Footprint for LANTIRN, JEIM, AIS

	Personnel		Support equipment (short tons)	
	CIRF	No CIRF	CIRF	No CIRF
☐ LANTIRN	4	12	0	22
■ JEIM	19	73	0.25	60
☒ AIS	7	24	0	41

RAND MG151-4.4

Table 4.2
CIRF Manpower Requirements: Actual vs. Planned

CIRF	Commodity	Actual Manpower	Planned CIRF Augmentees Assigned
Lakenheath	F-15 LRUs	5	7
Lakenheath (AEF/OEF)	F100-PW engines	8	8
Lakenheath (AEF only)	F100-PW engines	5	5
Lakenheath	LANTIRN pods	6	4
Spangdahlem	ALQ-131 ECM pods	7	7
Spangdahlem	F110-GE engines	7	6

The CIRFs also supported all of the ONW/OSW sortie requirements, as well as the unexpected OEF requirements. While meeting sortie requirements was the primary goal of CIRF operations, one of the test's secondary goals was to keep spare-item inventories above a zero balance at all times. The inventories remained at one or above at some units, but hit zero at others. Causes of the specific deficiencies, and the corrective actions taken, are described in the CIRF Test Report.[8]

C2 Achievements

The operational successes of the CIRF test resulted in large part from the success of the CIRF system's C2 network. Although the RSS was initially understaffed and needed augmentation to provide 24/7 support, its integrated structure enabled cross-functional analysis and allowed the CIRF to provide responsive support to the deployed units. Similarly, the common operating picture provided by the CIRF toolkit enabled effective decisionmaking at the RSS, the transportation hubs, and the CIRFs themselves.

Even when operational goals were in jeopardy, the CIRF system was able to adapt to meet the required sortie schedule. For example, while the system met the test plan's customer wait-time goals for LANTIRN pods, it fell short for engines and ECM pods. However, by measuring performance against the standards set in the test plan, and using incoming feedback effectively, the CIRF staff recognized these shortfalls, understood the interdependence of the systems supporting CIRF operations, and was able to compensate in other areas of support performance.

Because effective support depends on the interaction of several disparate systems—most notably, supply, repair, and transportation—it is possible to develop a tradespace of support options in which if one system falters, another may be able to pick up its slack. For example, during the CIRF test, the ECM pods repaired at Spangdahlem faced longer transportation times to the CIRF than desired (an average of 4.2 days vs. the 4-day target). However, the units had also deployed with one spare pod for every two aircraft deployed. They were therefore able to compensate for deficiencies in transportation performance and could maintain their sortie schedule. Similarly,

---

[8] Headquarters Air Force/ILMM, 2002, pp. 6–16.

on several occasions, F100 engines at the Lakenheath CIRF spent more time awaiting parts (AWP) and awaiting maintenance (AWM) than desired (an average of 2.7 days AWP and 1.4 days AWM, when the target was no time waiting for either parts or maintenance). However, because the units deploying during the CIRF test brought their "best" engines with them, F100 engines experienced a far lower removal rate during the CIRF test (2.33 removals/1000 flying hours) than their worldwide removal rate (5.48 removals/1000 flying hours). With fewer engines removed, the longer average customer wait time for each of these engines had less of an impact on operations.

Because support systems are so interdependent, the optimal removal rates, spares deployment levels, transportation times, and other support parameters depend greatly on interaction between the systems. As part of the CIRF test, RAND used a simulation model to define a support tradespace that would meet the operational requirements of ONW and OSW. Details of this analysis are provided in the appendix.

Challenges Faced
Despite the successes of the CIRF test, there were also notable opportunities for improvement.

Deployment Management. The CIRF staff faced challenges in deployment management. Because no augmentation UTCs had been defined at the beginning of the test, personnel instead needed to be pulled in by unit line number (ULN), forcing deployments to be planned at a much finer level of detail. Furthermore, to moderate the delays caused by the augmentation process, substantial time was spent trying to provide this added capability from personnel permanently stationed at the CIRF locations. It was also difficult to manage the 15-day rotations of the Air National Guard (ANG) augmentees. The frequent rotations led to rapid turnover of trained personnel, and a disproportionate amount of time devoted to paperwork and other costly activities that did not contribute to operations.

Transportation. Transportation was another key area in which problems were noted during the test. While the CIRF C2 system was able to adapt to most of the transportation shortfalls, the Air Force will ultimately need to deal with the problems found if it is to maximize the system's performance. For example, few items were transported in scheduled movements. Instead, transportation of engines to CIRFs, and all transportation to and from the aerial port of debarkation (APOD), was arranged as a need arose—usually when items failed or when they arrived at the APOD. This makeshift scheduling led to delays, and time-definite delivery suffered as a result.

CIRF transporters also faced challenges in moving ECM pods, which are classified. Ground transportation of the pods between Al Jaber and Kuwait City International Airport created force protection concerns because of the need for a classified courier and a security forces escort. At the end of the CIRF test, the Air Force recommended deploying maintenance capability to Al Jaber rather than relying on the transportation system.

Furthermore, the test plan did not contain well-defined policies on the modes of transportation that would move items to and from the CIRFs. USAFE was originally using a combination of trucks and C-130s to move cargo to the CIRF, mostly relying on trucks, but putting items on C-130s when the aircraft had excess capacity and could fit the items going to the CIRF. However, transportation routes for C-130s were unpredictable, and cargo waiting for an aircraft could at times have been shipped faster by truck. The resulting shipment delays continued until Tanker Airlift Control Center (TACC) reports highlighted the issue and relayed concerns to USAFE, who ultimately shifted to a truck-only policy. This experience highlighted an achievement of the C2 system's feedback loops, but it also underscored the need for better-defined transportation processes.

Command and Control. While the CIRF C2 system contributed significantly to the test's success, there were areas in which C2 could be improved. For example, although the CIRF toolkit facilitated the sharing of data across organizations, there was valuable information not incorporated. For instance, the portal did not contain information about the status of engines and pods in the repair process; it indicated only that they were being repaired and were not immediately available. As a result, units could not anticipate when their items would be returned. Furthermore, the reporting system was not centralized within the CIRF, and during the test there was no point of contact established for engine status. Consequently, deployed units were forced to contact several people in the propulsion flight line for information. This distracted CIRF personnel from their assigned duties and often resulted in conflicting reports when the same question was posed to more than one person.

Similarly, although the toolkit normally contains the location of each engine and pod, during the CIRF test it did not provide this information as a unit status report. Information was instead tracked by engine and pod serial number, which made it difficult to aggregate records to the unit level. As a result, it was difficult to provide feedback on a unit's capability or what its future needs might be. This, in turn, made it more difficult for the RSS to allocate resources effectively. The portal also provided very little information on changes to units' taskings. As a result, CIRF managers routinely had to react quickly to operational changes throughout the test. In addition, the Global Air Terminal Execution System (GATES) and Brio, the system and operating environment used in requirements forecasting, are currently under study to improve their capabilities. The ability of CIRF staff to predict cargo arrival depends on the accuracy of these systems.

Even when accurate feedback and forecasts were available, CIRF planners had difficulty using this information to revise operational and support plans. For example, if assets sent to the CIRF were missing components or had problems not included in the accompanying documentation, CIRF staff did not always have communication channels through which to follow up. In the event that discrepancies needed to be resolved before repair could proceed, the lack of accountability at the deploying units led to an increase in customer wait time. Lack of documentation also made it difficult to investigate potential issues of foreign object damage (FOD) or equipment abuse possibilities, and did not provide a way to incorporate them into policies and plans.

The lack of accountability in asset deployment is just one manifestation of poorly defined CIRF procedures. Although the RSS performed well as the decision authority and planners had developed a series of decision rules before the start of the test, the rules did not incorporate all of the scenarios that actually took place. Maintenance and part requirements were often renegotiated throughout the course of operations. Because a CIRF was often not prepared for these added requirements, additional capability needed to be deployed.

In addition to the difficulties encountered with forecasting and deployment management, planners also faced problems with the cross-cannibalization of CIRF wing assets. Although cannibalization was implemented frequently and reduced the amount of time items sat idle and waiting for parts, the process was not sufficiently standardized. When wings stationed at the CIRF locations gave up parts for cannibalization, their own home station support was degraded. Assets became tied up in AWP status, and tracking the funds of cannibalized parts became difficult. Furthermore, although LRUs belonging to the CIRF wings were authorized with the same JCS priority code as those of deployed units, this authorization was not universally understood by all shop personnel. The CIRF test showed that until a cannibalization process is formalized and CIRF wing assets are given the same priority as deployed assets, it will be difficult for the CIRF wing to expeditiously replace their components.

The funding process using AF Form 616 also caused significant delays during the CIRF test. Units deploying to ONW, OSW, or OEF that were using the RAF Lakenheath and Spangdahlem CIRFs were required by the CIRF CONOPS to establish an AF Form 616 account to pay for their repairs. The procedures involved with 616 accounts were time-consuming, labor-intensive, and difficult to manage. Furthermore, when multiple units were using the CIRFs, several 616s needed to be opened before each unit could deploy and had to be closed again at the end of its deployment. This was not an easy process on either end. CIRFs sometimes needed to order assets on their own accounts and be reimbursed later. Complications in both the ordering and reimbursement processes often resulted in further delays.

In addition to procedural difficulties, the CIRF test uncovered discrepancies in the Air Force's command relationships. For example, the USAFE/RSS had the authority to distribute engines to both the EUCOM and CENTCOM theaters, even though CENTCOM was not a USAFE AOR. This occasionally led to confusion and hindered comprehensive decisionmaking because the USAFE/RSS was not familiar with all the issues of the CENTCOM (U.S. Central Command) theater.

Conclusion: CIRF Test Planning and Results

Despite the challenges faced, the CIRF test demonstrated that with proper planning, CIRFs can successfully support steady-state operations, using fewer repair resources and requiring a smaller footprint than maintenance facilities deployed to FOLs. The test also showed, however, that support depends on effective intratheater distribution and C2, which ensure that items can be effectively allocated and delivered, even as priorities change.

Although the USAFE CIRFs being tested supported only SWA deployments, the issues raised in the test were expected to have lessons for combat support worldwide. The CIRFs of the AF/IL test were developed as standing organizations, with clearly defined augmentation procedures to support deploying units. These augmentation procedures, and the CIRF's successful support of OEF, raise the possibility of a larger CIRF network to support operations in CONUS and overseas. In the next two chapters we will discuss some of our analytical results in developing a CIRF support tradespace and assessing the centralized ownership concept. In the final chapter, we discuss steps that might be taken for a larger-scale CIRF implementation.

CHAPTER FIVE

CIRF Support Tradespace Development

The CIRF test was successful in verifying many of the advantages of maintenance forward support locations and highlighting their requirements. However, practical tests are constrained by the operational scenarios being exercised and the inability to control many of the parameters needed to test the range of FSL capabilities. As discussed in Chapter Four, the CIRF test's success largely resulted from understanding how the distribution and maintenance systems interacted to support operations and the use of this information in setting standards for system performance. To supplement the Air Force's operational analysis of FSL performance, RAND used a series of analytical models to test and verify several of the CIRF performance standards. This chapter describes the use of these models, explores several components of CIRF support, and determines a tradespace of how each component must perform to ensure successful support of operational requirements.

Methodology: Simulation Modeling

To estimate system performance, we used the Engine Maintenance Systems Evaluation (EnMasse) simulation model,[1] developed by RAND to assess CIRF repair capabilities. Our analysis focused on

---

[1] For a detailed description of the model, see Amouzegar and Galway, 2003.

F100-100 engines and ECM pods, which were of greatest concern to the Air Force because of their relatively high failure rates and frequency of use. However, the EnMasse parameters could be modified to study the use of other commodities.

We simulated a single base, flying either F-15s (for F100-100 engines) or F-16s (for ECM pods). The model uses the units' flying programs, the expected removal rates of engines and pods, and the service time, as measured by the times engines and pods spend in transit, awaiting parts (AWP), awaiting maintenance (AWM), and in work (INW). In this model, as diagrammed in Figure 5.1 for engine maintenance, sorties are "flown" based on a given peacetime utilization (UTE) rate or on predetermined surge/sustain sortie rates. After each sortie, engines and pods are inspected and may be removed and

Figure 5.1
EnMasse Model of Engine Repair

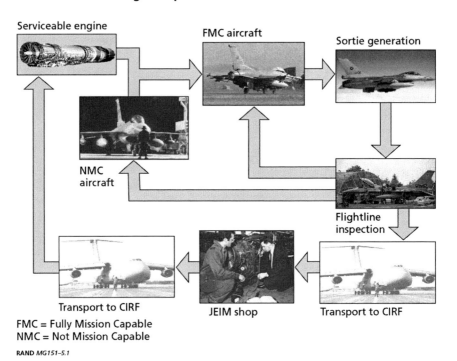

FMC = Fully Mission Capable
NMC = Not Mission Capable

RAND *MG151-5.1*

sent for maintenance based on the item's removal rate. If an item is removed, either it is replaced with a spare on hand or, if no spare is available, the aircraft is designated as not mission capable (NMC) until the part is replaced (fully mission capable [FMC]). Removed items are shipped to the CIRF, where they are repaired. In this model, AWP measures include cross-cannibalization. Finally, repaired items are returned to the unit as serviceable spares. The model was developed to show the daily spares performance over the duration of a deployment. The Air Force has set an operational standard of maintaining at least one serviceable spare engine and pod at each unit at all times. Having these spares available ensures that operations will not be affected by a failed component, since there would be a spare available to replace the failed one. We therefore defined our "performance standards" as the minimum performance level that must be attained (i.e., the longest transportation time, the highest repair rate, or the smallest spares deployment) to maintain a spare level of one or more at all times.

Each simulation was run at least 100 times, to provide a reasonable estimate of the system's performance.

Scenarios

Both the F100-100 and the ECM models were based on 90-day, steady-state scenarios, similar to ONW and OSW. Details on sortie lengths and durations, engine and pod removal rates, and CIRF performance (transportation times, maintenance times [AWP, AWM, and INW], etc.) are based on data recorded during the CIRF test and were defined as follows:

F100-100 Engine

The F100-100 model was based on a single F-15 base with 12 primary airctaft assigned (PAA) and six spare engines deployed, flying at a steady state of six four-hour sorties per unit per day. This was meant to represent the 1st fighter wing's (1FW) performance in the CIRF test. Our original analysis used a removal rate of 2.33 per 1000 flying hours, based on 1FW performance in the CIRF test.[2]

The CIRF performance parameters in our model were based on CIRF test operational experiences,[3] as shown in Table 5.1

Transportation times to and from the CIRF, varied as part of our analysis, ranged from four to eight days in either direction. When the transportation time was fixed, it was held at six days, as was achieved in the CIRF test.

Table 5.1
CIRF Repair Parameters, F100-100 Engine

	INW	AWP
Min	3	0
Max	11	9
Average	5.5	3.2

ALQ-131 ECM Pod

The ALQ-131 model was based on a single F-16 base with 10 PAA and five spare engines deployed, in accordance with the Air Force 50 percent spare pod guideline. The unit flew at a steady state of five 3.09-hour sorties per unit per day. Our analysis used a rate of 12.05 removals per 1000 flying hours, based on data collected in RAMPOD.

The repair performance parameters for ECM pods were also based on CIRF test data, as shown in Table 5.2

Transportation times to and from the CIRF, varied as part of our analysis, ranged from three to eight days in either direction. When the transportation time was fixed, it was held at four days, as was achieved in the CIRF test.

---

[2] The 1FW flew 2784.4 aircraft-hours over the six months of the test, or 5568.8 engine-hours. Over the six months of the test, the 1FW experienced 13 engine removals for either major or minor maintenance, for an overall removal rate of 2.33/1000. This removal rate is less than half the worldwide rate of 5.48/1000, the effect of which will be explored later in the chapter.

[3] One outlier engine was excluded.

Table 5.2
CIRF Repair Parameters, ALQ-131 ECM Pod

	INW	AWP
Min	0.5	0
Max	9	8.5
Average	3.23	2.03

Repair Assumptions: CIRF Operations

As previously stated, we assume that in a steady-state scenario, the CIRF would perform only minor maintenance. In an MRC scenario, we assume the CIRF would perform major maintenance as well as minor, but that the CIRF would be augmented to accommodate the additional workload. We also assume that the AWP and INW times would be similar for both the MRC and the steady-state scenarios. Table 5.3 shows the CIRF repair times for each engine type in our analysis.

For each scenario, we incrementally varied the initial spares deployments and the transportation time to and from the CIRF. Because the removal rates of the F100-100 engine observed in the CIRF test were less than half of those of the worldwide fleet, we also examined the robustness of CIRF performance to removal rate. The goal was to show how the CIRF would perform as it was implemented on a larger scale and the engine removal rate came closer to that of the worldwide fleet. None of these analyses was intended to

Table 5.3
CIRF Repair Parameters, F100 Engine Family

Engine Type	Maintenance Type	AWP	INW
–220	Minor only	0	5.88
–220	Major + minor	0	5
–229	Major + minor	1.5	7
–100	Minor only[a]	3.2	5.5

[a]One outlier engine was excluded.

determine a single "right" removal rate or transportation time, but rather to help planners understand how the repair, transportation, and supply systems work together. We performed a comparable analysis with the ECM model.

These variations tested several support concepts that are key to the CIRF system. Since total customer wait time (CWT) is equal to the sum of its individual components, the spare-level impact of increases in transportation time is comparable to the impact of similar changes in time spent on the flight line, repair time at the CIRF, AWP time, or any other portion of CWT. Although the optimal tradeoff of these individual component times has not been determined, studying the impact of transportation time (and of CWT in general) on operations helps to determine what total CWT might keep spares inventories at acceptable levels, thereby setting an upper bound on the individual component times.

Similarly, variations in removals may be representative of several system components, including flying program (where additional flying hours would result in additional removals), effectiveness of repair (where better quality repair would result in fewer removals), or operations tempo (optempo) (where, under surge or sustainment flying, units might be more inclined to "push" their existing equipment, resulting in fewer removals per flying hour). Finally, changes in spares deployment are an important aspect of the support tradespace, because the effect of a long CWT or a high removal rate may be alleviated by deploying additional spares.

Results: F100-100 Engine

For the F100-100 engine, our model revealed that CIRF performance throughout the simulated deployment was very robust to changes in transportation time. This finding resulted primarily from the low removal rate observed in the CIRF test—2.33 removals per 1000 flying hours (or engine removal approximately once every nine days). Furthermore, the repair time achieved in the CIRF test (AWP+AWM+INW) for the F100-100 was more than 10 days, so the transportation time to the CIRF was only a small part of overall CWT. As a result, small changes to transportation time had little effect on daily spares levels. Even doubling the one-way transportation time from four days to eight results only in a 50 percent increase in overall CWT (from 18 to 26 days), and the average daily spares level is maintained well above the one-spare threshold throughout the conflict. Figure 5.2 illustrates the daily level of serviceable spares for a range of transportation time (tt). The average sortie duration (ASD) is about four hours and engines are removed at a rate of about 2.33 per 1000 flying hours. In this scenario, the number of serviceable spares falls in the early days of the operation, reflecting the time required for the CIRF to return serviceable engines to the units. The curves then flatten out as serviceable spares are returned to the unit and a balance is reached between engine failure and repair. The combination of on-hand spares and CIRF production keep the levels of

Figure 5.2
Impact of One-Way Transportation Time on Spares Performance, F100-100 Engine

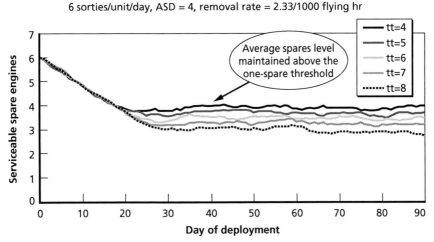

6 sorties/unit/day, ASD = 4, removal rate = 2.33/1000 flying hr

the serviceable spares above the one-spare threshold throughout the 90-day rotation.[4]

Initial spares deployment, on the other hand, has a greater impact on average daily inventory. Holding transportation at six days and the removal rate at the 2.33/1000 hours (approximately what was achieved during the CIRF test) resulted in an additional daily spare for each additional initial spare in the inventory. Figure 5.3 illustrates the results as the initial spares deployment is changed from four to eight.

As stated earlier, the F100-100 removal rate achieved in the CIRF test was far lower than the worldwide removal rate. This result was attributed largely to the fact that deploying units generally plan to bring their "high-time" engines (i.e., those that are not due for scheduled maintenance) with them, and can therefore reduce removals over the course of their rotation. However, as the CIRF concept is

Figure 5.3
Impact of Initial Deployment on Spares Performance, F100-100 Engine

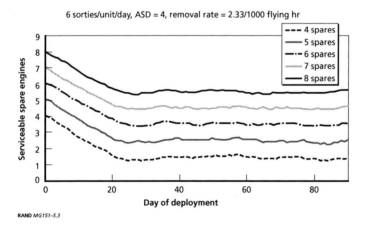

RAND MG151-5.3

---

[4] It should be noted that this is an average result. It is possible that for any given day the number of spares fell below one. Our focus, in this research, was on the overall performance of the system but it may be of interest to compute the daily probability that at least one spare asset is available.

implemented on a larger scale, and more engines are deployed, the removal rates achieved will approach the worldwide rate of 5.48 removals per 1000 flying hours.

F100-100 CIRF performance is far more sensitive to incremental changes in removal rate than to changes in transportation performance or in initial spares deployment. Removal-rate changes are the only one of the three that impact the CIRF workload (and therefore may also impact the CIRF augmentation plan) as well as the CWT or unit spares levels. The incremental effect of removal rate (RR) on spare engine inventories is illustrated in Figure 5.4.

Results: ALQ-131 ECM Pod

Compared with the F100-100 engine, the ALQ-131 pod has a much higher removal rate (12.05 removals per 1000 hours). As a result,

Figure 5.4
Impact of Removal Rate on Spares Performance, F100-100 Engine

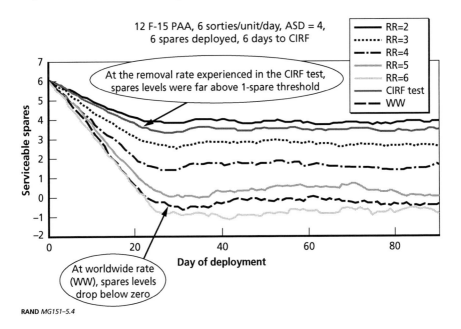

even with fewer aircraft in the unit, far more removals per day are expected for pods than for engines. With more pod removals, there is a greater workload at the CIRF. By extension, changes in transportation performance have a greater effect on stock levels for pods than for engines. As was experienced in the CIRF test, the ECM units in our model fell below the targeted threshold level of one spare with the travel time of four days to and from the CIRF (i.e., the unit at times faced a "zero balance" of spares, with the possibility that aircraft would need to fly without pods). At this target transportation time, the average inventory drops below one at approximately day 40 (see Figure 5.5).

Holding transportation constant at four days, the unit would maintain a positive spares inventory if it initially deployed with an extra spare (six instead of five). As was the case with engines, pod removal rates are low enough that successful repair of the ALQ-131 is more sensitive to changes in spares deployment than to changes in one-way transportation time. The result is illustrated in Figure 5.6.

Figure 5.5
Impact of One-Way Transportation Time on Spares Performance, ALQ-131 Pods

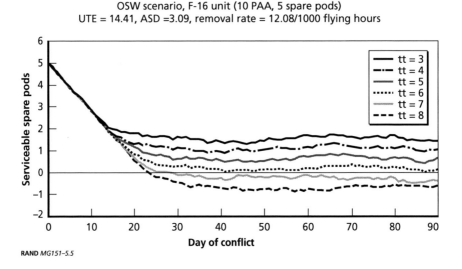

OSW scenario, F-16 unit (10 PAA, 5 spare pods)
UTE = 14.41, ASD =3.09, removal rate = 12.08/1000 flying hours

Finally, we held transportation time constant at four days, and spares deployment constant at five spares to represent deployment and performance levels of the CIRF test, and incrementally varied the pod removal rate (see Figure 5.7). As was the case with the F100-100 model, inventory levels are significantly higher as the removal rate is held lower. However, unlike the F100-100 scenario, the effect of incremental changes in removal rate is not the most influential factor in determining daily inventory levels. Because the removal rates are high, moving from 12 to 13 removals for pods (less than a 10 percent increase) is not as significant a change as moving from two to three removals per 1000 flying hours for engines (a 50 percent increase). Furthermore, with a higher removal rate, and more pods removed, increases in transportation time become far more significant than they were in the F100-100 scenario.

Figure 5.6
Impact of Initial Deployment on Spares Performance, ALQ-131 Pods

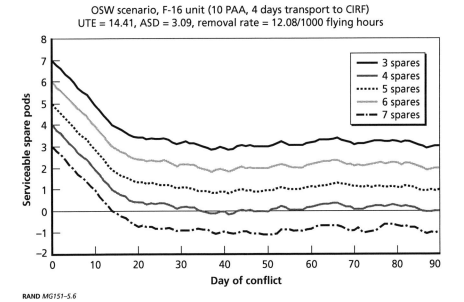

OSW scenario, F-16 unit (10 PAA, 4 days transport to CIRF)
UTE = 14.41, ASD = 3.09, removal rate = 12.08/1000 flying hours

RAND *MG151–5.6*

Figure 5.7
Impact of Removal Rate on Spares Performance, ALQ-131 Pods

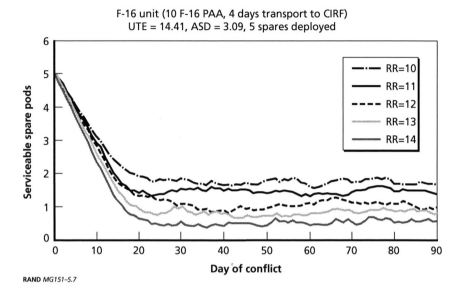

RAND *MG151–5.7*

As shown above, centralized maintenance for both engines and pods is robust to some changes in operational environment but sensitive to others. Furthermore, the extent of the sensitivity to one change is also dependent on the performance of the rest of the system. Therefore, if one element were to perform less effectively than expected (e.g., if transportation capacity were reduced, increasing CWT), another element can be adjusted (e.g., deploying additional spares to stem the increased CWT) to balance out performance.

Conclusions from Tradespace Development

The EnMasse model allowed us to explore potential scenarios beyond those experienced in the CIRF test. By varying operational and performance parameters, both independently and in combination, we were able to study how the CIRF can best respond to changing conditions. Simulation modeling enabled us to explore conditions not experienced during the six months of the CIRF test and to set parameters that best relate support performance to operational goals.

The scenarios tested with EnMasse demonstrated that successful CIRF operations are dependent on a synergy of several support processes. As the component removal rates increase, changes in transportation performance have a greater impact on operational performance. Likewise, the deployment of additional spares can help units to compensate if either repair or transportation performance falters.

Simulation modeling can also be used in the analysis of ongoing operations. For example, if CIRF staff is notified of an upcoming deployment, or the spares deployment level or availability of transportation is likely to change, the system can be simulated to reflect changing conditions. Based on the model results, planners can then determine whether to deploy additional spares, or reduce CWT, in order to maintain operational performance levels.

CHAPTER SIX

Conclusions and Recommendations: Further ACS Implementation

Centralized Repair in Today's Operating Environment

Recent years have shown that combat support has become an increasingly important dimension of Air Force operations and that intermediate maintenance—a vital part of combat support—offers great opportunity for improvement through short-term changes. The CIRF test has demonstrated that overseas CIRFs can carry out the intermediate-maintenance functions required to support steady-state operations, with a smaller deployment footprint than that for decentralized maintenance.

The CIRF test also demonstrated that a C2 structure with clearly defined organizations, operational and support plans, and standards for performance enables CS systems to adapt to changing conditions. With such a structure in place, planners can recognize when support performance is threatening to undermine operational readiness and can take corrective actions—either by adjusting the process that has gone off course or by changing a corresponding process.

Although the CIRF test examined performance in only a single region and for a specific set of deployments, the real-world success of the overseas CIRFs in the test suggests that RAND's comprehensive

ACS vision is viable and can meet the Air Force's current needs. The positive performance of the system during the test indicates that the Air Force should continue to develop and test other system configurations.

Further Development of ACS Concepts

Operating environments and their support needs are likely to change from one deployment to the next. The support configuration used in the CIRF test may not always be the one best suited to the operating environment. Other configurations—for example, one that incorporates CONUS CIRFs—may better enable the Air Force to deploy quickly and provide the best support. With the high premium on quick response that today's security realities require, the Air Force will also need to continue to refine the C2 and distribution systems on which the ACS system depends, and it may also adopt a policy of centralized ownership to provide the required flexibility.

CONUS CIRFs

With substantial input from the MAJCOMs, the Air Force is developing plans to examine centralized intermediate repair for F-15 avionics components, F100 and F110 engines, TF-34 engines, and ECM and LANTIRN pods. This plan could potentially reduce the number of repair facilities in CONUS from 145 locations to as few as 21.

The Air Force has also examined possible further implementation of CONUS CIRFs. The Air Force Logistics Management Agency (AFLMA) has begun a series of analyses examining the centralization of intermediate repair for F-101 engines (used in the B-1 bombers). Although the results of these analyses are still in their preliminary stages, they indicate that CONUS CIRFs may successfully support ANG B-1 units, which are consistently manned at peacetime levels and do not require UTC commitments. The stability of these manpower requirements permits consistent staffing and easier implementation of a centralized facility.

CONUS CIRFs, however, raise several challenges. The distance between the operating bases and the CONUS CIRFs would increase reliance on transportation; by moving repair capability to CIRFs, CONUS units would no longer be able to repair items at their home stations. Additional spares would be needed to fill the longer pipelines. Furthermore, the establishment of CONUS CIRFs could have political implications—the movement of personnel and resources to and from CONUS bases will affect the funding states receive and operating bases will become smaller as repair capability is moved to CIRFs.

The concept of CONUS CIRFs has been debated for six years, from the first discussions of the ACS in 1997 to the AF/IL efforts in 2003. After extensive analysis, the Air Force has determined that CONUS CIRFs have the potential to drastically reduce requirements for repair resources while maintaining the level of support to which combat and training units are accustomed.

C2 Network

The vital role of C2 in the success of the CIRF test validated the importance of C2 in the complete ACS system. However, despite the operational successes of the test, several complications with the C2 system were uncovered. They centered on two key issues: resource allocation and information sharing. We propose several modifications to Air Force organizations, information systems, and process definitions to resolve some of the shortfalls that became evident during the test.

While communication and mutual understanding between operational and support personnel are key to successful C2, the links between the two communities are not always clear-cut. For example, even if the CIRF and the supporting transportation and supply systems run as planned, the possibility exists that with an unusually high engine or pod failure rate, an FOL might still lose spares and reach a zero balance. Similarly, the CIRF could fall short of its performance goals without affecting readiness at the FOLs. Because the links between operations and support are not easily quantified, it is important for the CIRF to be part of a C2 network that keeps planners for all parts of the repair process informed of the state of operations. A flexible process is required for planning and execution that can accommodate unexpected changes in operational needs and performance as conditions evolve. This flexibility requires centralization of planning in a group of support organizations that can clearly communicate with the operational community and among themselves. Such communication will allow support planners to stay abreast of operating conditions and allocate resources accordingly.

Organizational realignment of combat support, at the MAJCOM and globally, will improve the allocation of resources across competing organizations. During the CIRF test, while policies and procedures were well defined in the CONOPS and test plan, there were complications in defining the chain of command. ONW and OSW were under two different commands (EUCOM and CENTCOM, respectively), and the USAFE/RSS needed to allocate resources to both commands, despite not having a comprehensive picture of CENTCOM operations. The need to define the roles of CIRF organizations became further evident during Operation Iraqi Freedom (OIF). Whereas the RSS played a pivotal C2 role during the CIRF test, organizational changes to the RSS before OIF, such as the removal of maintenance and transportation personnel to carry out unit-level tasks, resulted in a loss of the systemwide view that helped the test succeed. USAFE/LGM took charge of CIRF operations in OIF and maintenance performed well throughout the conflict, but there was little ongoing analysis on how maintenance performance was influenced by supply and transportation performance, and how this interaction affected the end users, the combat units. It was therefore difficult to alter support plans and performance to respond to operational needs.

The implementation of an effective ACS C2 system is also dependent on feedback and information sharing between different organizations and on the smooth transition of information at each stage of an operation. The CIRF test permitted sharing of information, but there was also important information omitted. CIRF operations could be improved by expanding the toolkit to include more details on the status of items in repair and to aggregate item status reports to provide information by unit. Furthermore, procedures should be instituted to communicate deployment changes to the RSS, which will consider this information in its decisionmaking. For steady-state operations, the AEF center and MAJCOMs should inform the RSS or the Operational Support Center (OSC) when deployment packages change, through the CIRF toolkit or other established reporting channels. The RSS and OSC can then task additional augmentees as needed, and the CIRF will be able to allocate spare items accordingly.

Distribution

The ACS system, particularly if it relies on maintenance centralized away from the theater of operations, is dependent on an effective distribution system. The CIRF test, and operations that have followed it, have identified several distribution issues that need to be resolved. These issues may be classified into two general categories: C2 and in-transit visibility (ITV). The C2 problems may be minimized as CIRF concepts are further formalized, processes become better defined, and organizations are developed specifically for CIRF planning and execution activities. Recommendations stemming from assessments of OIF also emphasize the institutionalization and formal consideration of CIRF concepts in transportation planning. This consideration does not necessarily require CIRF items to take on a higher transportation priority; it simply calls for the Air Force to address the specific needs of CIRF operations when allocating resources, and to use different decision rules than those used for non-CIRF commodities.

ITV can be improved by formally incorporating CIRF concepts into transportation planning. Further developing information systems such as the CIRF toolkit and centralizing information about CIRF items within organizations will provide clear channels for communicating necessary in-transit information to those who need it.

Centralized Ownership

RAND's ACS vision proposes that common ownership of CIRF commodities will facilitate centralized intermediate maintenance because it will allow CIRF staff to send repaired items to the units where they are needed most. During the CIRF test, the Air Force overrode existing unit-ownership policies to allocate resources on an exception-only basis. This created a number of complications, in that units were frequently denied the use of items they needed but did not "own," or were forced to deal with bureaucratic procedures to be granted "exception" item allocations. Repair was also halted at times, if test stands were already in use when a "higher-priority" item came in for repair. Instituting a formal centralized-ownership policy would provide several advantages. It would ensure that units with the most stressing operational requirements receive the items they need, while reducing the overhead issues involved with an exception-only allocation policy. Centralized ownership would also eliminate the need to pull a part from repair to fix an equivalent item that might be owned by a higher-priority unit. It would reduce the pipeline time and improve spares levels at units with the greatest operational need for engines and pods, because these units could be allocated any appropriate items that came out of repair without waiting for "their own" part to be completed. For engines, centralized ownership would also facilitate module matching, which would reduce the likelihood of delays due to parts.

Despite these expected benefits, maintenance and operating units throughout the Air Force have greeted the concept of centralized ownership with some resistance. Because engine repair is cycle-time driven, units have raised concerns that unless they have "their own" engines returned to them, they might receive engines with less time available before the engine's next scheduled maintenance. The units then face the possibility of sending their engines for repair more frequently than they had planned and jeopardizing their ability to meet their sortie schedule. In addition to the potential operational implications of unexpected engine failures, the changes in engine availability and repair needs would complicate units' budgeting of repair funding. Without the guarantee that they would have their own engines returned to them, the units would have greater difficulty projecting what their repair needs would be and developing a budget to support these needs. Questions have also been raised about the quality of repair, how repair of centrally owned parts would be funded, and what the C2 requirements would be.

Although the Air Force did not fully implement centralized ownership of engines or pods during the CIRF test, the CIRF planning staff recognized the benefits such a policy could provide. AF/IL asked RAND to examine how centralized ownership might fit into a larger CIRF implementation and to quantify the extent to which it would increase spare item availability. With a better understanding of the benefits provided by centralized ownership, the Air Force could then determine whether it was worthwhile to address the units' concerns, establish the required C2 infrastructure, and implement a centralized ownership policy. RAND's simulation analysis compared the impact of centralized and unit ownership policies on unit inventory levels and operational readiness. The analysis included an examination of the concerns raised by the units and the infrastructure requirements for optimal implementation of centralized ownership. The results of the simulation study demonstrate that centralizing ownership of CIRF commodities has the potential to balance inventories across units and improve overall readiness. If engines and pods continue to break at the same rate and the CIRF continues to operate at the same pace, the total number of available spares will be approximately the same under either policy. But if either the rate of breakage or the pace of operations changes, the story will be different. For example, if the sortie schedule of a particular unit becomes more demanding, having the flexibility to reallocate spares will enable the Air Force to give that unit precedence so that it will be more likely to have a spare on hand when needed. Furthermore, under centralized ownership, units may be able to tap into a larger spares pool than the assigned War Reserve Materiel (WRM) levels. Not only will these additional spares improve the readiness of the engaged, higher-priority units, but they can be reallocated at the end of a deployment.

The Air Force has recognized the benefits allowed by centralized ownership, but it has also determined that implementing a centralized ownership policy is a significant undertaking. They have therefore taken steps toward such a policy by implementing a rotating CIRF engine pool (CEP). This pool provides the responsiveness of a remove-and-replace allocation structure and reduces the number of 616 funding forms in use. Currently, the Air Force is developing a CONOPS for the CEP, which was implemented in Operation Iraqi Freedom. The clearly defined processes and flexibility provided by the CEP during the recent conflict helped to offset any transportation difficulties.

Structural Considerations in CIRF Planning

As CIRF-based maintenance systems are implemented in more locations in support of more operations, there will be several strategic factors to consider. A primary concern will be the military's strategic priority, which will dictate whether the appropriate maintenance strategy for a particular operation uses overseas CIRFs, CONUS CIRFs, or decentralized maintenance. If CIRFs are used, strategic needs will also dictate where the facilities should be located and what support systems should be in place. In the event that the Air Force does use a CIRF-based system, planners will need to coordinate deployments of combat units to the theater of operations with deployments of supporting units and equipment to the CIRF locations. Planners will also need to decide how these resources will be shared over the duration of a conflict. A flexible CS infrastructure, and analyses such as the tradespace development discussed in this report, will aid in this coordination.

Most important, the support structure and decision rules put in place to support a set of operations must be reevaluated periodically. Strategic plans change, as does resource availability, and the CS support infrastructure needs to be flexible enough to adapt to changing conditions. The ACS network proposed by RAND and the Air Force will enable the Air Force to achieve the highest level of flexibility to support evolving operations.

Recommendations

Based on the above discussions, we therefore make the following recommendations:

The USAF should continue to explore the option of using overseas CIRFs in conjunction with CONUS CIRFs. This would allow units to share repair resources, thereby consolidating maintenance operations and reducing personnel and equipment. Furthermore, if the resource savings were great enough, the Air Force might have enough equipment available to move some overseas in peacetime as well as wartime. This would reduce airlift needs when units deploy for a contingency, particularly at the beginning of deployments when airlift is in greatest demand.

The USAF should realign its support organizations and establish an Operational Support Center (OSC) at each MAJCOM. This will provide the needed all-inclusive view of CS throughout an operation. OSCs will serve as regional hubs for monitoring, prioritizing, and allocating theater-level CS resources, and they will also provide mission support and establish movement requirements within the theater. To keep resource allocations aligned with global operational priorities, the OSC should report to the theater Air Force Forces/A-4 Rear, and have visibility of theater resources and the ability to work with Air Force and Joint-service communities. When two OSCs are competing for scarce resources, that allocation decision should be elevated to an Air Force Combat Support Center that can coordinate the resources of competing MAJCOMs. To enable it to perform this function, the Combat Support Center should have responsibility for providing integrated weapon system assessments across commodities. An analysis cell for intertheater allocations could be co-located with the ACC/RSS.

All organizations involved with CIRF planning and allocation should have clear channels of communication with deployed units and the CIRF. The CSC2 should also have clearly defined communication channels with each of the OSCs. Furthermore, planning and allocation organizations with the potential to deploy to the theater should have clearly defined UTCs and augmentation packages to streamline the deployment processes.

To improve access to toolkit data and other information, CIRF planners, the RSS dealing with CIRF operations, and deployed units should establish points of contact that can provide all parties with a common operating picture. CIRF staff should have channels through which to stay informed of upcoming deployments as well as feedback channels for cases where deployments are incomplete or the deployed assets are broken or not properly documented. Units can then correct their deployment packages and explore root causes of the deployment problems.

The USAF should consider centralized ownership of engines and pods.[1] To successfully implement the centralized ownership initiative, a decision authority must be established and the proper command and control structure instituted to allocate spares dynamically as units' needs change. Furthermore, a centralized budgeting and funding process may be needed to enable centralized repair and decisionmaking and address the units' concerns regarding budgeting for uncertain repair needs. This transformation requires further analysis.

---

[1] See the appendix for a detailed assessment.

Centralized Ownership Analysis

Centralized maintenance, successful throughout the CIRF test, has the potential to reduce the resources required for overseas intermediate repair. In this appendix we explore another option for CIRF management—centralized ownership. We first describe the differences between the centralized ownership policy and the current unit ownership policy, and then show the differences in operational performance under each of those options. Finally, we examine some of the management issues that may either impede or enable centralized ownership.

Policy Descriptions

Base Case: Unit Ownership

Under the unit ownership policy used during the CIRF test, each unit owns its own engines and pods, and pays for these items to be repaired. In peacetime, for CONUS operations, engines are allocated according to the annual propulsion requirements system (PRS) process, and most intermediate-level repair of engines and pods takes place on base. When the units deploy, all spares that have been marked for deployment move with them to the FOLs. When engines and pods break overseas, they are sent to the theater CIRF, where they are repaired in the order in which they are received.[1] If high-priority items are inducted for repair, and there are no open repair stands, items currently in work might be taken off the stand and put on hold so the higher-priority items can be fixed. Removing an item from the test stand mid-repair is not advisable; it is done only when deemed absolutely necessary and is not considered in our model. If there are spares available at the FOL, the broken item is replaced immediately with another unit-owned spare. If there are no spares remaining, the unit must wait for a repaired item to come back from the CIRF. It is possible for one unit to borrow from another, but this is generally done informally, on an exception-only basis, and is also not modeled in our analysis.

Excursion Case: Centralized Ownership
Under a centralized ownership policy, spares would be owned and managed by a single independent entity for each commodity, not tied to a particular unit. Although CONUS repair is likely to remain at the individual base level, and CONUS spares are therefore not likely to be drastically reallocated, deploying units will face a dramatic policy shift.

Instead of deploying all war reserve spares from CONUS to their FOLs, units would deploy with only enough spares to cover the CWT pipeline to and from the CIRF (see Figure A.1). The remainder of the spares would deploy to a central location, most likely the CIRF, where they could then be sent to units as they are needed. The total number of spares in the theater need not change.

We examined a case in which the number of spares in the theater would change. Under a centralized management policy, the RSS or designated decision authority has the option of tasking nondeployed units to "donate" engines to the CIRF to support deployed operations. We explored the impact that this "spare tax" would have on overall effectiveness.

_____
[1] Although the "first in, first out" rule is generally applied, priority may be given to certain units.

Figure A.1
Comparison of Unit and Centrally Managed Deployments

Unit Managed Deployment   Centrally Managed Deployment

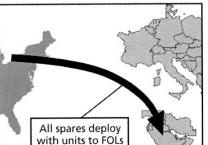 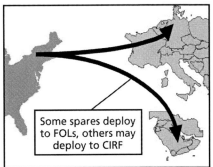

Under centralized ownership, as under unit ownership, engines and pods that are removed in the theater are sent to the CIRF for repair and are replaced by spares in the unit's safety stock. In the centralized ownership case, unlike in the unit ownership case, there will also be a pool of spares at the CIRF. If the CIRF pool has spares when a unit's part breaks, one will be sent immediately to replenish the unit's safety stock.

As in the unit ownership case, parts are repaired at the CIRF in the order they are received. Under a centralized ownership policy, however, spares would be considered interchangeable, so they need not be returned to the unit that originally sent them. Instead, each unit would have a "target inventory level" set to accommodate its flying patterns and expected failures. When items come out of repair, they would be allocated to the unit furthest below its target level.

In our models, the target levels that form the basis for spares allocation were determined using an algorithm called the Multi-Echelon Technique for Recoverable Item Control, or METRIC.[2] METRIC is designed to minimize system backorders—represented by aircraft without engines or pods when they are needed and subject

---

[2] Sherbrooke, 1968.

to inventory constraints. METRIC calculations are based on a number of factors, including:

- Expected failures (as estimated from flying programs and break rates)
- Transportation time from units to the CIRF
- Repair and transportation time from the CIRF
- Number of spares available systemwide.

We assumed a dynamic allocation of inventory when setting our target levels, to reflect the fact that relative flying patterns shift during an MRC but not during a steady-state scenario. In an MRC, units deploy according to different schedules, and deployments and surges are staggered. Although the dynamics of this method place greater demands on the command and control of the spares allocation system, we expected that using it instead of unit ownership or a less dynamic common ownership policy would significantly improve the system's responsiveness.

Simulation Methodology

To assess the differences between the centralized and unit ownership policies, we modified the EnMasse model discussed in Amouzegar and Galway (2003) to include allocation decisions under centralized ownership, the ability to store inventory at the CIRF, and the ability to distinguish between F-15 and F-16 engines. We simulated MRC scenarios for the F100-229 and the F100-220, as well as a steady-state scenario for the F100-220, under both the unit ownership and centralized ownership policies. As in the tradespace analysis, our principal measure of effectiveness was spares availability over the course of the conflict.

Assumptions: CIRF Operations

The revised model provides the option to swap engines from the F-15 MDS to the F-16. The F100 family of engines is built for either an

F-15 or F-16 aircraft body, so it is possible to reconfigure engines and move them between the F-15C/D, F-15E, and the F-16C/D. However, since each MDS is designed for different missions (suppression of enemy air defenses, air-to-ground, etc.), engines wear differently on each airframe. Furthermore, since F-16s have only one engine, while F-15s have two, F-16 engines are held to a higher quality standard to reduce risk to the aircraft. As a result, discrepancies related to Time Change Technical Orders (TCTOs) and configurations do not make swapping engines between MDS an attractive option.

Under the current policy, the CIRF returns repaired items only to the unit that originally sent them in. Because each of these units flies only a single MDS, we assume that there is no need to reconfigure engines. Under centralized ownership, however, the opportunity to swap engines between MDS might significantly increase the number of spares available to a unit when they are needed. Therefore, while we assume that the TCTO and configuration issues would preclude the reconfiguration of engines under a steady-state scenario, we also assume that during an MRC, when the need for engines is likely to be more pressing, that the CIRF would convert and swap engines as needed.

Operational Scenarios
As previously stated, one of the CIRF's key advantages is that provided the facility is sufficiently manned, repair can begin as soon as broken engines and pods arrive. We therefore assume that repair can be performed as needed, with parts AWM only when the CIRF is already working to capacity.

Throughout the CIRF test, planes flew their ONW/OSW missions at an AEF steady-state level, with no surges. Although there was additional flying, and additional CIRF demand generated, as a result of OEF, we have limited our ONW/OSW analysis to the steady state as a model for future operations. Surges in flying are considered in our MRC analysis instead.

Throughout the CIRF test, the CIRF performed only minor maintenance, leaving major maintenance to be done in CONUS. Minor maintenance is defined as tasks that do not require fan duct rollback and keep engines on schedule for their next phase inspections. Major maintenance involves fan duct rollback and leaves the engine acceptable for a complete phase inspection interval. We assume that in an MRC the CIRF would perform major as well as minor maintenance. However, because the CIRF staff would be augmented to operate around the clock, the CIRF can also handle the increased workload in less time than the bare-boned CIRF handled only minor maintenance. All of our calculations, both steady state and MRC, were based on AWP and AWM times observed in the CIRF test. Likewise, the distribution of transportation times used in our model was based on times observed in the CIRF test. We assume that these distributions included the time spent preparing and waiting for transport, as well as the time actually spent in transit, and would be similar for an MRC scenario.

Sample Case: The F100-229

Operational Scenario. As an example, we give the results of an MRC model for the smallest fleet, the F100-229. Its deployment schedule is shown in Table A.1.

We assume that each unit flies at its surge rate for the first 10 days and at a sustain rate for the remainder of the conflict. F-15 and F-16 flying schedules are provided in Table A.2. The parameters provided are notional (unclassified).

The engine removal rates used in our model are based on Air Force estimates. We assume that in peacetime F-15 engines fail at a

Table A.1
F100-229 Deployment Schedule: SWA
MRC Scenario

Day	Aircraft Deployed	Spare Engines
10	48 F-15E	16
21	24 F-16	6
24	12 F-16	3

Table A.2
F-15/16 Operational Data

	Flying Schedule			Sortie Duration		
MDS	Peacetime (UTE)	Surge	Sustain	Peacetime	Surge	Sustain
F-15	18	1.6	1.0	1.5	3.0	3.0
F-16	19	2.0	1.0	1.5	2.5	2.5

rate of 3.83 failures per 1000 flying hours and F-16 engines fail at a rate of 4.62 failures per 1000 flying hours. Removal rates are reduced during an MRC, under the assumption that engines will be "pushed harder" in more dire circumstances, and that faults that might result in a removal in peacetime would not necessarily do so in wartime. The reduction rates for both the surge (27 percent) and sustain (18 percent) periods are also based on Air Force estimates.

The distribution of repair times used in the engine analysis is based on times observed in the CIRF test. The transportation times are also based on times observed in the CIRF test and shown in Table A.3. We assume that these distributions include the time spent preparing and waiting for transport, as well as the time actually spent in transit, and would be the same for an MRC scenario.

According to our simulation results, inventory levels at each FOL drop in the first days of flying, as units fly at their surge rates and engines break but are not yet repaired. As engines are repaired,

Table A.3
One-Way Transportation Distributions Achieved in CIRF Test Results

Time	Engine Type	Min	Max	Average
To CIRF	F100-229	9	9	9.00
From CIRF	F100-229	5	10	7.50
To CIRF	F100-220	4	8	5.75
From CIRF	F100-220	3	19	7.75
To CIRF	F100-100	2	8	5.29
From CIRF	F100-100	3	7	4.14

the units shift to their sustainment-flying schedule, and the CIRF continues to produce engines. Inventory levels recover and eventually stabilize. As shown in the series of graphs, the two F-16 FOLs perform better under the centralized ownership policy ("pooled" lines in Figure A.2–Figure A.6), while the larger F-15 units perform better under unit ownership. Under centralized ownership, the larger units face a drop in performance (as shown in Figure A.5) in order to supply the smaller units, which have fewer spares initially allocated. However, while the units' spares levels may necessitate cannibalization in some instances, none of the units drops below the threshold at which they begin to lose sorties.

As shown in Figure A.6, there is virtually no inventory stored at the CIRF. Because engines are allocated to the CIRF only when all of the units are fully stocked (i.e., to their target levels), this implies that the F100-229 engine, when allocated according to the PRS numbers,

Figure A.2
Spares Performance, 24 F-16s and 6 Spares

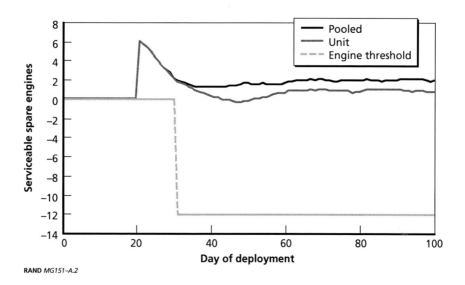

Figure A.3
Spares Performance, 12 F-16s and 3 Spares

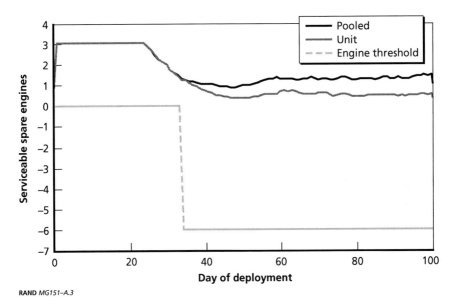

RAND MG151–A.3

is a scarce resource. Deploying more spares from the engaged units or using loaner engines from other units could provide a more robust safety stock, reducing the risk of holes in aircraft.

Under a centralized ownership policy, the decision authority would task units to send spare engines to the CIRF even if the units' aircraft are not deploying. Although some of the units' readiness to perform training missions would suffer, the move would drastically improve responsiveness at the CIRF and readiness in theater. In our initial scenario, with no additional spares deploying, the CIRF stock was zero throughout the conflict. As a result, when an engine broke, the unit, at the least, had to wait for an engine to be repaired, reallocated to that unit, and sent from the CIRF. If there were no engines in the repair queue at the time of a failure, the unit would have to wait for an engine to be sent in, repaired, reallocated, and sent back.

Figure A.4
Spares Performance, 48 F-15s and 16 Spares

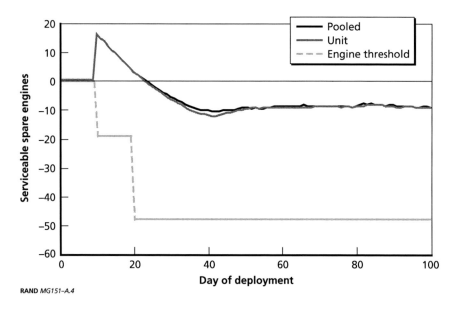

A stockpile of spares at the CIRF would shorten the CWT required. With this safety stock, a spare could be sent to a unit as soon as its engine breaks, eliminating the wait for an engine to be repaired. This is reflected in the FOL inventory graphs in Figure A.7–Figure A.11—where the initial inventory dip is smaller and is recovered more quickly, as more spares are prepositioned at the CIRF.

As shown in Figure A.11, the initial spares inventory is depleted in the first 30 days of the deployment, as engines break at the units but have not yet gone through the repair cycle. Once repaired parts begin to come out of repair, the inventory begins to recover and eventually reaches a steady level. In this case, at least 10 additional spares must deploy to maintain a CIRF inventory of at least one for the duration of the conflict and to then be able to respond to breakage as it occurs.

Figure A.5
Spares Performance, 33 F-15s and 6 Spares, Peacetime Unit

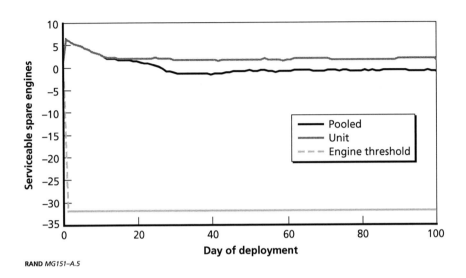

Figure A.6
CIRF Stock, F100-229 Engines

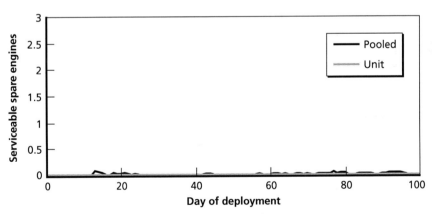

Figure A.7
Spares Performance with Additional Spares Deployed, 24 F-16s and 6 Spares

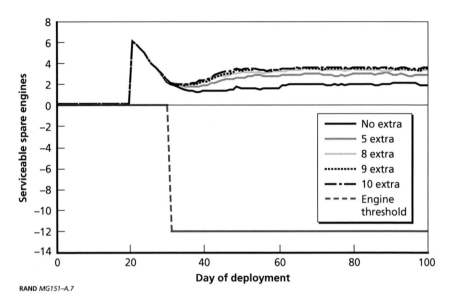

RAND *MG151–A.7*

Implementation of Centralized Ownership

As shown above, a centralized ownership policy has the potential to balance inventory levels across FOLs and support units when they are experiencing the greatest demand. However, proper implementation of centralized ownership will be the key to its success.

Unit Concerns

Concerns about centralized ownership revolve largely around uncertainty in the quality of the parts that units will receive. Since centralized maintenance was first introduced, units have been concerned that without the "pride in ownership" of the parts they are repairing, maintenance personnel may not repair engines to the standard that they would if they were repairing their own. This concern has been addressed by maintenance staff, who insist that the quality of their repair is completely separate from the issue of ownership.

Figure A.8
Spares Performance with Additional Spares Deployed, 12 F-16s and 3 Spares

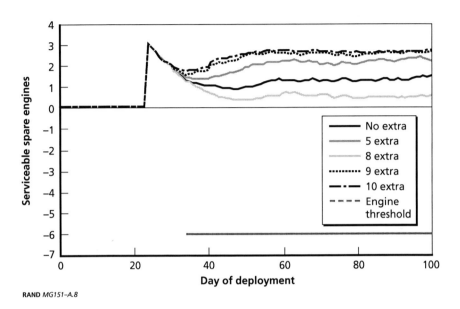

There is also concern that, for example, a unit may send an engine with 1,000 remaining cycles to the CIRF, only to have that engine allocated to another unit and an engine with only 500 cycles returned to the original unit. Receiving an engine that is due for repair earlier than expected is likely to complicate units' budget forecasts, since most repair budgets are forecasted based on the mean time between failures (MTBF). This is less of a concern for pods, because electronic devices are effectively "zero-timed" every time they are repaired. However, under the principle of Reliability Centered Maintenance (RCM), maintenance staff thoroughly inspect and repair incoming engines, rather than simply fixing the fault for which the engine was sent to the CIRF. This proactive maintenance strategy helps to ensure the quality of all repaired engines.

Furthermore, centralizing ownership of engines and pods may also result in the centralization of repair forecasts. If CIRF repair funding came through the supported MAJCOM, the need for unit-level estimates, and the error in these forecasts, may be alleviated.

Figure A.9
Spares Performance with Additional Spares Deployed, 48 F-15s and 16
Spares

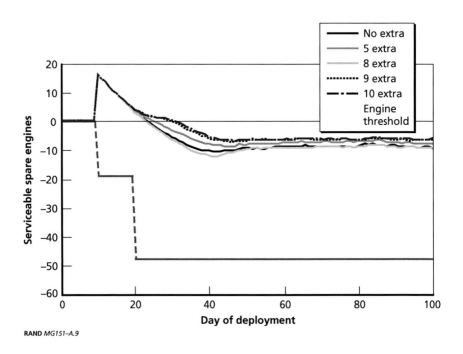

RAND *MG151–A.9*

Command and Control Needs

For the decision authority to operate effectively, there are several C2 requirements. First, if the RSS remains the CIRF decision authority, and therefore is responsible for funding decisions, it must have accurate visibility of the status of all spare parts. Systems must monitor the flying schedules and spare parts inventories of each unit to permit central forecasts of repair needs. This information, combined with the proper command authority, will enable dynamic allocation of repaired parts and the resulting improved performance.

Figure A.10
Spares Performance with Additional Spares Deployed, 33 F-15s and 6
Spares, Peacetime Unit

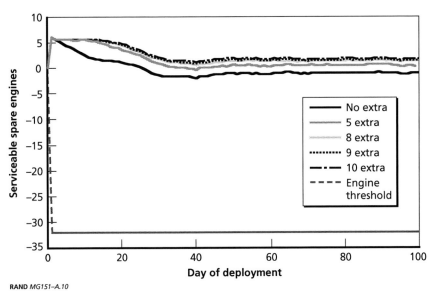

Figure A.11
CIRF Stock with Additional Spares Deployed

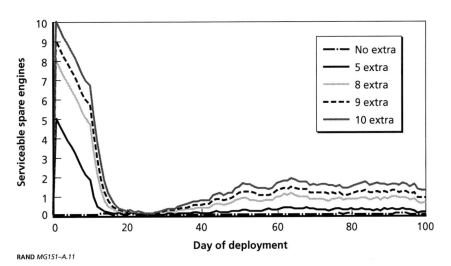

In addition, the USAFE/RSS currently coordinates, facilitates, and prioritizes repair at the CIRFs, but it tries not to interfere with "production," or the actual repair operations. If CIRF operations were to switch to a centralized ownership policy, the RSS would require improved C2 capability. Currently, when units deploy, the CIRF operations staff is augmented but the RSS planning functions are not. Furthermore, visibility of assets and of centralized priorities is maintained manually, and through informal communication. The CIRF often overrides RSS decisions on prioritization of assets and the order of repair. Under a centralized ownership policy, the RSS would need greater augmentation in its planning functions, as well as the authority to allocate spares from one unit to another. Institutionalization of CIRF C2 and development of CIRF doctrine will aid in acceptance of the new repair and management policies.

Budget and Funding

Another issue that must be addressed for successful implementation of centralized ownership is the development of a proper funding process. As discussed earlier, this process is currently extremely fragmented. Units pay for their own repairs, are responsible for their own budget forecasts, and must separate these forecasts based on what they will need at their home station and what they will need from the CIRF. They must then provide their 616 forms 30 days prior to deployment to ensure a smooth transition. The CIRF, meanwhile, is responsible for the fuel and oil used in repair of each unit's engines. All of these expenses are then reimbursed from the Overseas Contingency Operations Transfer Fund (OCOTF).

If all engines and pods are to be managed by a single authority, the funding process will need to be revised. Because items will be shared among all units, it will be impossible for units to know which engines and pods will be assigned to them or what their repair needs will be. Furthermore, if units no longer "own" their engines and pods, they will not be expected to fund their repair. Intermediate repair will therefore need to be funded on a larger scale, where demand can be gauged and budgets forecasted theaterwide.

For example, if the MAJCOM were to open a single 616 account that applies to all its units, forecasts could be made on a larger scale and cause fewer delays resulting from lack of funding. It would also alleviate the pressure on the CIRF home unit to fund equipment and fuel used in testing, and reduce the extent to which CIRF home capability is compromised.

Added Benefits of Centralized Ownership

In addition to the added demands that centralized ownership of spares places on the CIRF system, there are benefits beyond the spares performance already described. For example, under the current unit ownership policy, engines and pods are repaired in the order in which they are received. However, because each unit is bound to get its "own" repaired parts back, the capacity of the CIRF is more of a constraint than it would be under centralized ownership. If the CIRF is already working to capacity and a high-priority order comes in, either the order must wait for a repair stand to become available or a part in work must be pulled from repair to accommodate the new part. This results in a delay in processing or disrupts the ongoing repair, with the potential for problems when repair on the removed part is resumed. Under centralized ownership, on the other hand, parts in repair are not tied to the units that sent them. As a result, if a unit has a high-priority need for an engine or pod, the next FMC part to become available can be sent immediately.

Centralized ownership and centralized storage of spare engines also facilitate module matching, a procedure designed to reduce engine removal rates. When modular engines are repaired, the maintenance staff attempts to match the cycle times on each module in the engine. This procedure reduces the delays caused by an engine being removed for scheduled maintenance of one component and then removed again for maintenance of another component a short time later. Currently, because individual units own their own engines, each unit is limited to modules from its own fleet, even if another suitable engine is also in repair at the CIRF. Under common ownership, modules could be swapped from any available engine.

Bibliography

Amouzegar, Mahyar A., and Lionel A. Galway, *Supporting Expeditionary Aerospace Forces: Engine Maintenance Systems Evaluation (EnMasse): A User's Guide*, Santa Monica, Calif.: RAND Corporation, MR-1614-AF, 2003.

Amouzegar, Mahyar A., Lionel A. Galway, and Amanda Geller, *Supporting Expeditionary Aerospace Forces: Alternatives for Jet Engine Intermediate Maintenance*, Santa Monica, Calif.: RAND Corporation, MR-1431-AF, 2001.

Berman, Morton B., M. J. Carrillo, J. M. Halliday, N. Y. Moore, and J. E. Peterson, *Combat Benefits of a Responsive Logistics Transportation System for the European Theater*, Santa Monica, Calif.: RAND Corporation, 1981 (Government publication; not for public release).

Berman, Morton B., I. K. Cohen, and Stephen M. Drezner, "The Centralized Intermediate Logistics Concept: Executive Summary," Santa Monica, Calif.: RAND Corporation, internal draft, 1975.

Carrillo, M. J., and Raymond Pyles, *F100 Engine Capability Assessment in PACAF: Effects on F-15 Wartime Capability*, Santa Monica, Calif.: RAND Corporation, 1982 (Government publication; not for public release).

Cohen, I. K., T. Lippiatt, R. Richter, and R. J. Hillestad, "An Evaluation of the Performance of the PACAF Centralized Intermediate Logistics Concept," Santa Monica, Calif.: RAND Corporation, internal draft, 1977.

Craven, Wesley Frank, and James Lea Cate (eds.), "The Army Air Forces in World War II," *Men and Planes,* Vol. 6, Chicago, Ill.: The University of Chicago Press, 1955.

Feinberg, Amatzia, Hyman L. Shulman, Louis W. Miller, and Robert S. Tripp, *Supporting Expeditionary Aerospace Forces: Expanded Analysis of LANTIRN Options,* Santa Monica, Calif.: RAND Corporation, MR-1225-AF, 2001.

Feinberg, Amatzia, Robert S. Tripp, James Leftwich, Eric Peltz, Mahyar Amouzegar, Russell Grunch, John Drew, Tom LaTourrette, and Charles Robert Roll, Jr., *Supporting Expeditionary Aerospace Forces: Lessons from the Air War Over Serbia,* Santa Monica, Calif.: RAND Corporation, MR-1263-AF, 2002.

Futrell, Robert Frank, *The United States Air Force in Korea, 1950–1953,* New York: Duell, Sloan, and Pearce, 1961.

Galway, Lionel A., Mahyar A. Amouzegar, Richard Hillestad, and Don Snyder, *Supporting Expeditionary Aerospace Forces: Reconfiguring Footprint to Speed Expeditionary Aerospace Forces Deployment,* Santa Monica, Calif: RAND Corporation, MR-1625-AF, 2003.

Galway, Lionel A., Robert S. Tripp, Timothy L. Ramey, and John G. Drew, *Supporting Expeditionary Aerospace Forces: New Agile Combat Support Postures,* Santa Monica, Calif.: RAND Corporation, MR-1075-AF, 2000.

Headquarters AFLC, *Project Pacer Sort, Final Report,* June 30, 1967.

Headquarters Air Force, *Maintenance Management,* AFM 66-1, 1958.

Headquarters Air Force/ILMM, "CIRF Test Report," DRC Contract Delivery Order K1102BJ2055, June 21, 2002.

Headquarters USAFE, *Personnel and Equipment Listings for Deployment of Units,* USAFE Manual 400-2, Vol. 1B, September 30, 1965.

Keaney, Thomas A., and Eliot A. Cohen, *Gulf War Air Power Survey: Summary Report,* Washington, D.C.: U.S. Government Printing Office, 1993.

LaTourrette, Thomas, Donald Stevens, Amatzia Feinberg, John Gibson, and Robert S. Tripp, *Supporting Expeditionary Aerospace Forces: Forward Support Location Options,* Santa Monica, Calif.: RAND Corporation, 2003 (Government publication; not for public release).

Leftwich, James A., Amanda Geller, David Johansen, Tom LaTourrette, Patrick Mills, C. Robert Roll, Jr., Robert Tripp, and Cauley von Hoffmann, *Supporting Expeditionary Aerospace Forces: An Operational Architecture for Combat Support Execution Planning and Control*, Santa Monica, Calif.: RAND Corporation, MR-1536-AF, 2002.

Moody, Colonel Howard A., "Rear Area Maintenance," Letter to Brigadier General Alkire, Deputy for Materiel, Headquarters FEAF, May 24, 1952.

Nelson, Major Carl G., "REMCO: A Korean War Development," *Air University Quarterly Review,* Vol. 6, No. 2, 1953.

PACAF Deployment Support Manual, PACAF Manual 400-1, December 1, 1967.

Peltz, Eric, Hyman L. Shulman, Timothy L. Ramey, and John G. Drew, *Supporting Expeditionary Aerospace Forces: An Analysis of F-15 Avionic Options,* Santa Monica, Calif.: RAND Corporation, MR-1174-AF, 2000.

Rainey, James C., Mahyar A. Amouzegar, Beth F. Scott, Robert S. Tripp, and Ann M. C. Gayer (eds.), *Combat Support: Shaping Air Force Logistics for the 21st Century*, Air Force Logistics Management Agency, 2003.

Sherbrooke, C. C., "METRIC: A Multi-Echelon Technique for Recoverable Item Control," *Operations Research,* Vol. 15, No. 6, 1968, pp. 985–110.

Sweetman, Bill, "Expeditionary USAF Sets Course," *Jane's International Defense Review,* Vol. 33, 2000.

Tactical Air Command, *Organization and Mission—General—Organization of Tactical Air Command Units*, TACM 20-1, Langley Air Force Base, Virginia, March 1962.

_____, *Mobility Planning*, TACM 400-1, Langley Air Force Base, Virginia, September 1967.

Tripp, Robert S., Lionel Galway, Paul S. Killingsworth, Eric Peltz, Timothy L. Ramey, and John G. Drew, *Supporting Expeditionary Aerospace Forces: An Integrated Strategic Agile Combat Support Planning Framework,* Santa Monica, Calif.: RAND Corporation, MR-1056-AF, 1999.

Tripp, Robert S., Lionel A. Galway, Timothy L. Ramey, and Mahyar Amouzegar, *Supporting Expeditionary Aerospace Forces: A Concept for*

Evolving the Agile Combat Support/Mobility System of the Future, Santa Monica, Calif.: RAND Corporation, MR-1170-AF, 2000.

U.S. Air Force, *DoD Dictionary of Military and Associated Terms*, Joint Publication 1-02 (JP 1-02), April 12, 2001.

_____, *Air Force Basic Doctrine*, Air Force Doctrine Document 1 (AFDD-1), September 1, 1997.

_____, *EAF Factsheet*, June 1999.

USAF Logistics Transformation Team report (USAF/ILM-T), April 2001.

Waters, Jack W., *The Development of Logistical Support Policies for Tactical Fighter Aircraft*, United States Air Force Air War College, 1968.